HUNTING

The Chase *by A. Ackermark, 1894*

HUNTING
A Portrait

Anne Holland

LITTLE, BROWN

A *Little, Brown* Book

First published in Great Britain in 2003
by Little, Brown

A CIP catalogue record for this book
is available from the British Library.

ISBN 0 316 86069 7

Designed by Wilson Design Associates
Printed and bound in Great Britain
at The Bath Press

Little, Brown
An imprint of
Time Warner Books UK
Brettenham House
Lancaster Place
London WC2E 7EN

www.TimeWarnerBooks.co.uk

A WISH

O, fame is a fading story
And gold a glitter of lies,
But speed is an endless glory
And health is a lasting prize;
And the swing of a blood horse striding
On turf elastic and sound
Is joy secure and abiding
And kingship sceptred and crowned.

So give me the brave wind blowing,
The open fields and free,
The tide of the scarlet flowing,
And a good horse under me;
And give me that best of bounties:
A gleam of November sun,
The far spread English counties,
And a stout red fox to run.

Will Ogilvie

Contents

Author's Note & Acknowledgements

The personalities and hunts described in the following pages represent a portrait of hunting as a whole, from the small hunt and the 'backroom boys' to the ducal packs and their fine estates, where all genuine followers are welcomed equally.

The patchwork quilt that makes up the fabric of rural Britain sees hunting across almost all parts of it, from the busy South-East to the wilds of Northumberland, the craggy fells of Cumbria to the Shires of Middle England, the moors of Devon and Cornwall to the arable land of East Anglia. It is the same story in Ireland.

What shines through time and again among the characters portrayed is their sheer love of the countryside, of friends, of horses and hounds – and especially of the sport of hunting itself.

People hunt for many different reasons. For some, it is the love of a horse or the challenge of crossing a stiff country; for others, it is watching the hounds at work; for some, it will be the making of a young horse, or for qualifying point-to-pointers; for the 'footies', those stalwart followers on foot, bike and car, it is the hunting, not the ride; to certain farmers, it is dispersal or riddance of a pest; for the professionals, it is more than a job, it is a way of life; for most, it is a mixture of many of these things. However followed, it is the thrill of the chase.

I would like to thank all those who have freely given of their time to help with the compilation of this book, and to apologize for not being able to fit in so many more who are equally worthy of inclusion.

To all who have given their time and help, and especially to Bob Champion; photographers Des McCheane and Jim Meads; and Alan Samson and Catherine Hill at Little, Brown, for their support and enthusiasm.

Also to George Alcock, Sidney Bailey, Gary and Julie Barber, James Barclay, Roger Bennett, Mary Bridger, Arianne Burnette, Elizabeth Bury, Tamsin Castle, Ross Coles, Bob Collins, Colin Day, Lady Dulverton, Edward and Janet Eames, Tom Egan, Rodney Ellis, Ian Farquhar, Michael Farrin, Joan Gilchrist, Andrew Gunther, Rex Hancock, Tim and Tessa Holland, Jo Jewell, David Jones, Oliver Langdale, Martin Letts, Stan Luckhurst, Baroness Mallalieu, the late Roger Manning, Sarah Milne, Sally Mitchell, Tom Normington, James Norton, Michael Osman, Stephen Petitt, Bryan Pheasey, Dick Power, Colin Reynolds, Chris Ryan, Jane Ryan, Thady Ryan, Diana Scott, Linda Silverman, John Stafford, Patsy Smiles, Roy Tatlow, Robert Vallance, Rob Watts, Jeremy Whaley, Patrick Wild, Mary Wilson, Steve Wilson.

Finally, my thanks to those kind South Islanders of New Zealand who arranged horses and beds for me, before my trip there was aborted.

Foreword by Bob Champion

I have found Anne's book fascinating. So much of it reminds me of my younger days and of the wonderful, unforgettable personalities that populate the hunting world.

A lot of steeplechasing jockeys, myself included, come to National Hunt racing via hunting and this experience makes them horsemen as well as jockeys. My involvement with the ponies, the people and above all with the sport itself, have given me a huge amount of pleasure, not only as a young boy, but all through my life. Certainly hunting was of great benefit to me, and I consider myself very lucky to have come from seven generations of huntsmen. When I was a boy Dad was hunting the Cleveland, so that's where I started. Since then, I have hunted wherever I have been living, including America.

Put simply, hunting is good for the countryside. This is something that comes over through Anne's pen very clearly, and she writes with great affection and wonderful detail about hunting all around the British Isles, as well as further afield. I love the flow of her book. She writes evocatively and with enthusiasm. She does not need to 'put the case for hunting', since this comes over time and again through the people and hunts she writes about. She ends with a moving personal story that for many will portray her strength of feeling for hunting and the people, horses and hounds within it.

I remember riding alongside Anne, probably longer ago than she cares to recall. We were both racing in a steeplechase on a sweltering hot August day at the pretty Sussex track of Fontwell, the result long forgotten. But, as I was all too aware then, while jockeys necessarily have a sell-by date, we can keep on hunting into much older age. And that is what we must fight to keep doing. This is a book that will be enjoyed by a far wider audience than diehard hunting men and women, and should be a compulsory read for a good many politicians, too. I have no doubt its many readers will enjoy it as much as I have.

Bob Champion, Newmarket, June 2003

I   Rally-Ho

It is the middle of Salisbury Plain.
A brisk, chill wind is blowing. Above,
the skylarks are singing. Underfoot, the
first signs of cowslips and violets are
appearing. Tall, rank grass still waves,
svelte-like, in the tracts that have been
ungrazed through the winter. There is
spring in the centuries-old, never
ploughed turf and the going is perfect.
An owl flies languidly out of a fir tree,
only slightly disturbed by the presence
of horses and riders.

It has been a quiet day, with little scent and fewer foxes, but it is still magical just to be out there, at one with nature, with horse and hounds and human friends. The gorse, usually a 'sure find', draws blank and we jog on. Suddenly, Lady darts left, her nose intently to the ground and then that first melodic cry of a find. She is swiftly joined by Rascal and Governor and Gantry, and before long the whole pack is as one, in full musical cry, the most stirring sound on earth. The huntsman blows the 'gone away', adding to the symphony. The riders stop their chattering and gather up their reins, hearts pounding, ready to follow.

'Charlie' (the fox) has jumped up in front of hounds but soon his speed distances him from them. Where the grass is shorter he is clearly visible to the human followers. The hounds don't look up, instead their noses are steadfast to the ground, following the scent in the centuries-old fashion that nature has blessed them with.

The old, retired racehorse stretches across the turf, hooves pounding. He is back at Cheltenham – but not quite, for suddenly there is a check, or maybe a quick sidestep in full gallop to avoid a hole, for a third eye and a fifth leg are two attributes he has acquired in retirement. A hat is raised aloft and pointed towards Sidbury Hill. There, just before he reaches the cover of the trees, we can see Charlie again. He pauses, looks round, lopes on unhurriedly, well ahead of his pursuers, and disappears.

It has been a marvellous hunt, led by a pilot who is fit and strong and healthy, and able to procreate more, unlike the poor mangy specimen creeping about in the gorse earlier for whom hounds had rendered a service by dispatching him instantly. We hack back across the Plain towards Nine Mile River and its thick thorn coverts and abundant wildlife. How could anyone wish to take this away?

OUR HERITAGE

This is our heritage; the far-flung grass,
The golden stubble and the dark-red moor;
Men pass and perish as the swift years pass,
But wide and windswept still the fields endure.

This is our heritage; the love of sport,
A fair ambition and a friendly strife,
The rivalry of farm and camp and court,
The keen endeavour of a clean, hard life.

The hoofs of horses on the trampled lea,
The crash and rattle of the broken rail
Where the first flight ride reckless, knee to knee,
And bold men face the dangers of the vale.

The cry of hounds, the holloa and the horn;
The lean red shadows where the foxes run;
To these and all their challenge we were born,
And these we leave behind us, sire to son.

This is the heritage that none can take,
The gift we hold, the gift we give again,
And this the spirit that no Time can break,
So long as England and her fields remain.

Will Ogilvie

London, Sunday, 22 September 2002

Early morning sunshine filters through the gently changing leaves; there is a ribbon of white mist lingering in the valley bottom; the horses have been fed, the dogs walked, and the cottage secured. On the short journey to the local market town one coach has already passed, heading out to pick up a group of shooters from the nearby estate. Approaching the car park, people in country clothes are converging from every direction.

From all corners of Great Britain, as well as Ireland (4,000), France (300), Australia and America (400), people are making their way to the unfamiliar streets of London: 407,791 of them in total – an all-time record – to march for 'Liberty and Livelihood'. The threat to hunting is the catalyst but country life in general is felt to be at stake, as the hunting thread is a part of the whole country tapestry.

A number more, after enduring all-day journeys and delays, are told they are too late for the authority-imposed 6 p.m. deadline and turn away, dejected. Many others are necessarily left behind, milking the cows, tending the country chores, doubling up for those who are away. Thousands more, including the very old, the infirm or too ill to walk, and those who are abroad – some 2,000 from New Zealand alone – have signed up to affirm that they are 'marching in spirit'.

Coach drivers have been given different routes into the capital to try and minimize congestion, but still there are delays. There are two separate march routes, yet there are so many of us that it takes 2 $^1/_2$ hours simply to reach the designated starts: one from Hyde Park and the other from Blackfriars.

Whistles blow, horns blare and thousands cheer and wave as babies and toddlers in pushchairs sleep on, oblivious. Policemen accept Liberty and Livelihood badges pinned to their lapels and smile benignly; they are old hands at this and know there will not be crowd trouble. The two columns – two mighty, winding rivers – merge into one mightier yet, a slow-moving, seething mass of human beings, meandering towards the last lap down Whitehall, like two 200,000-strong armies. Fittingly, as we file pass the Cenotaph, the whistles and cheers and horns stop, in

respectful silence for those who died fighting to preserve our freedom – our freedom.

Then it is a short walk past the officials counting heads at the finish. Dispersal means another long walk, for some as far as Battersea Power Station, to the homeward-waiting coaches and more unfamiliar urban traffic jams. Would we be listened to this time?

Although 22 September was the biggest rally, it was by no means the first. That distinction goes to the march in 1949 organized by a group that became known as the Piccadilly Hunt. In early February of that year, 315 MPs supported a private members' bill designed to ban hare coursing and stag-hunting, mistakenly believing these sports to be the domain solely of the privileged classes.

Some farmers, including Leonard Bennett from Worcestershire and Harry Johnstone and Geoffrey Milne from the Cotswolds, were bemoaning over a mug of beer the threat to their liberty so soon after the war. They were determined not to be reduced to playing tiddlywinks on a Saturday afternoon. 'We've helped to feed the nation, hunting is our only fun, and if this bill becomes law it will be the thin edge of the wedge' is what they said, recalls Leonard's son, Roger, who was six at the time.

They enlisted nearly fifty local farmers, hired two charabancs and, at 5 a.m. on 28 February 1949, journeyed to London. They hired horses from the stables at Knightsbridge, and rode off down Piccadilly, up Regents Street and Oxford Street to Hyde Park Corner, distributing leaflets as they went and carrying a large 'Farmers Protest' banner.

The leaflets explained that the farmers were protesting against the bill that 'is trying to stamp out our heritage'. They explained that, as farmers, they were well used to killing insects so that fruit could grow and rabbits and moles, pigeons and rooks to protect corn. 'If you take away our field sports, what will you give us instead? Remember, we can't pack up on a Saturday afternoon and Sunday like the townsfolk.' They exhorted people to talk to farmers rather than believe supposed 'appalling atrocities'. 'After all, we feed, study and nurse animals of all descriptions every day of our lives. We are not those cruel beasts you imagine. We know and understand Nature ... We did our best to feed you during the war; we are doing our best now. Are you going to turn on us and deny us our country sport?'

The protesters were hugely well received, with clippies and cabbies alike taking extra leaflets to give to their passengers. People asked numerous questions, many betraying complete ignorance of hunting and much else to do with the countryside.

More importantly, word came back that evening that the bill had been defeated by 214 votes to 101.

Some of the farmers had never been to London before and went off to sample the delights of Soho, while others found themselves, in full riding kit, invited to the Horse and Hound ball which by chance was taking place that night. It was a motley lot who returned to milk their cows at 5 the next morning, 24 hours after they had left home.

The protest made headlines in the London papers and much good fellowship was engendered.

The next year a reunion dinner was held and the group christened itself the Piccadilly Hunt. Its aim was to keep alive the spirit and passion shared for properly conducted hunting and field sports. Since then, a dinner has been held annually with usually a day's hunting somewhere in Britain as well. It has kept up political pressure and remains a force to be reckoned with and respected.

In 1991, a private members' bill was proposed to outlaw hunting, so Roger Bennett picked up the mantle vacated by his late father. He discussed a similar protest to that of 1949 with the Metropolitan Police, who insisted that no more than six horses would be allowed, and that protesters would only be able to walk up and down Park Lane. The numbers of would-be protesters grew from 500 to 1,500, to 5,000 and then 10,000, all by word of mouth.

Mr Winston Churchill out for a day with the Old Surrey and Burstow in 1949, hunting in protest at the proposal to ban the sport

Pressure to cancel the rally was put on Roger Bennett from eminent hunting men – Ronnie Wallace, known universally as 'god', and the hierarchy at the British Field Sports Society (BFSS), the forerunner of the Countryside Alliance, in particular. They were afraid it would cause riots by 'antis' pelting them and would give hunting a bad name. Roger put it to his committee. He had permission from the Metropolitan Police, after all. The Piccadilly Hunt committee was divided, but came down marginally on the side of a local demonstration at the Royal Showground at Stoneleigh instead. Two committee members resigned on the spot. The resultant highly successful demonstration at Stoneleigh, attended by 15,000 people, showed the BFSS, Roger believes, that a large London rally could be organized with confidence.

Six short years later, with another private members' bill in front of Parliament, that notion was put to the test with the rally in Hyde Park on 10 July 1997. It was attended by a staggering 120,000 people. As it is with hunting, so people from all walks of life took part, many of them catching their trains or coaches in the early hours, some from Scotland travelling through the night. For some, it was a first visit to London.

A highlight, which generated much response in the weeks leading up to the rally, was the core marchers, a group of die-hard supporters who set out in June to walk the whole way to Hyde Park from three starting points in Scotland, Cornwall and Wales, some 450 miles. The march was instigated by Mark Miller Mandy and organized by husband and wife team Charles and Chipps Mann. Throughout the march, the core walkers were joined by local people for one day in their own area, and everywhere they were put up at night by well-wishers.

The rally organizers had numerous eminent speakers ready but their delivery was fraught with behind-the-scenes difficulties, with various restrictions imposed by the Royal Parks Agency, some of them at the last minute. Earlier in the week, the organizers received a letter that appeared to cancel or alter many

The Hyde Park rally against the banning of hunting in July, 1997

People who hunt come from all walks of life: the Banwen Miners' Hunt pass through a working colliery

of the arrangements: it stipulated that the start must be put back from 11 a.m. to 12 noon, no music could be played through the amplification system, and the grandstand could not be constructed until the morning of the rally but must be up by 8 a.m. Inevitably, this meant some well-rehearsed musical numbers had to be dropped, but the pre-noon speakers still got their chance by announcing that they were warm-up artists.

There were many moments for people to savour on a day like this, from the makeshift loos in the bushes at a service station chosen by too many coaches for conventional conveniences – ladies to the left, gentlemen to the right – on the journey up to

the sight of 240,000 arms raised clapping above heads on the arrival at the rally of the core marchers. The organization was superb and a tribute to much that is still great in Britain. Halfway through, a delegation representing many different country sports and trades delivered a letter to 10 Downing Street, handed over by David Jones, huntsman of the David Davies pack in Wales.

The speeches themselves were truly rousing. David Jones declared the 'committed, courageous' walkers had walked 'for you and your children' and vowed, 'This is the last peaceful march and the last peaceful rally.' Jeremy Irons, the Oscar-winning actor, proclaimed that too many townspeople think of the countryside as 'an extended theme park' catering for 'little furry animals who speak as they do in Disney cartoons'. Neil Greatrex, President of the Union of Democratic Mineworkers, feared a ban on hunting would create as much social havoc as the closing of mines had done.

Sir Mark Prescott, a racehorse trainer from Newmarket, called the proposed bill 'mind-blowing moral juggling of an urban MP' who is 'a self-confessed competition angler', whose law would make it legal for a dog to chase a rabbit but not a hare. 'How is a dog meant to know the difference?' he asked, especially as the MP, when shown a picture of each, was unable to differentiate.

Roger Bennett, whose father had formed the Piccadilly Hunt to preserve hunting for his children and future generations, said, 'I hope that in fifty years, Hyde Park will be remembered as another watershed, so that our children can say the same about us.'

Willie Poole, the writer, memorably spoke that he was fed up with 'weirds with beards of both sexes … using and abusing me'.

But the speech that will forever be remembered by all came from Labour peeress Ann Mallalieu, a barrister whose favourite recreation is hunting on Exmoor. In her fruity, stirring voice, she said:

Farmers have left their haymaking, farriers have left their forges, racehorse trainers have left their runners at Newmarket. Doctors, nurses and vets have changed their shifts to be here. Judges have adjourned their cases for the day. Children have taken a day off school, and countless country firms and businesses have closed or are running on skeleton staff. People who are old and people who are ill have travelled many miles, some setting out before dawn. Others, as we've just seen, have been travelling for days through heat and rain, through pain and discomfort, from all parts of the United Kingdom and beyond. Great sacrifices have been made by many of the people who were determined to be here …

We have come here for one reason. We cannot and will not stand by in silence and watch our countryside, our communities and our way of life destroyed for ever by misguided urban political correctness.

This rally is not just about hunting. Many, perhaps most, of those here today don't hunt themselves. It is about freedom, the freedom of people to choose how to live their own lives. It is about tolerance of minorities – and, sadly, those who live and work in our countryside are minorities here today. And, above all, it is about listening to and respecting the views of other people of which you may personally disapprove …

Many of you spend your lives living and working with animals. You see birth and death at close quarters. It is you who take the hard decisions, you who bear the responsibilities day in, day out, and do the sheer hard work. It is an irony that this rally, composed as it is of people who know, love and live among animals, should be the target of abuse and vilification from those who claim to love animals but seldom have any practical knowledge of or direct responsibility for caring for them. The irresponsible seem to feel free and qualified to tell the responsible that they are – and I quote – 'barbaric sadists and perverts'. Well – there are an awful lot of perverts in front of me at the moment …

Tonight this park will empty. We will, all of us, be making our way home to all parts of the nation. We will go back to care for the animals and the countryside and its wildlife, of which we have been guardians for generations.

Don't forget us, or what we have done today, because we have made history. The countryside has come to London to speak out for freedom – and many from the towns and cities who understand our fears have stood here with us today. Today our voice has been one of calm reason. But make no mistake – the countryside is angry.

I hope that we are not on the eve of a battle. We do not want one. But if there is one, the countryside will fight back, and the countryside will win. To all those of you who have just given part of your lives to be here in Hyde Park, and particularly to those who have marched from all ends of our country, the best words that I can end with are those of another countryman, our greatest writer [Shakespeare], addressing a minority on the eve of another battle [Henry V at Agincourt], which was won against all the odds:

From this day to the ending of the world
But we in it shall be remembered,
We few, we happy few, we band of brothers.
For he today that sheds his blood with me
Shall be my brother; be he ne'er so vile,
This day shall gentle his condition.
And gentlemen in England now abed
Shall think themselves accursed they were not here,
And hold their manhoods cheap whiles any speaks
That fought with us …

At the end of the rally, the thousands wound their way good-naturedly back towards their coaches. They represented all walks and ranks of life, including many a middle-class, middle-aged lady who doubtless never imagined she would be participating in a public protest. There was nothing but praise from the police, unused to such polite protesters, lack of disturbance and absence of litter. As was so memorably coined: 'Would the last one out of Hyde Park kindly shut the gate.' Or, in hunting parlance, 'Gate, please!'

Just nine short months later, in March 1998, a conservative estimate of 250,000 people descended upon London again, this time in a well-orchestrated march along the London streets, once more with superb behaviour, followed by dispersal at Hyde Park and Underground trips back to various temporary coach parks.

In 1999, the theme was regional protests, to be attended by those whose jobs were on the line or likely to be affected. In the capacity of hunting correspondent, I attended the one at Bournemouth, during the annual Labour Party conference being held at that south-coast seaside resort. Not long after,

there was a coach trip to Exeter, where another well-attended march and rally received stirring speeches from eminent people, following a rousing blessing of and prayer for the event by retired hunting clergyman Rex Hancock, who brooked no fear in firmly hanging his colours on the hunting mast.

In December 2001, thousands more marched in Edinburgh in defence of Scottish hunting. All was in place for the 'big one', a march that was intended to take place on 18 March 2002, until the terrible foot and mouth epidemic put paid to it until 22 September 2002.

All of these protests, as we have seen, were undertaken in a tremendous spirit of camaraderie and goodwill, almost a sense of euphoria that with such numbers surely we would be listened to. The stirring rallying calls of eminent speakers will forever remain etched in the memories of those who heard them. These were uplifting occasions, undertaken with a mixture of muted anger at the threat to a way of life and a certain happiness brought by the banding together and belief in our cause. 'Listen to us' was chanted again and again, amidst a glorious cacophony of hunting horns, holloas and cheering Mexican waves. But did they listen?

The saddest day of my hunting life occurred on 23 March 2002. Two days before there had been a vote in the House of Commons coming out firmly in favour of a ban on hunting. It was near the end of the season; indeed, depending on the farming pattern, a good many hunts had already finished. We are not a smart hunt, not one of the elite, but small and friendly, doing no harm to anyone. We are farmers, housewives, teachers, local businessmen, one or two who work in London, and lots of enthusiastic children. Our meet was at the home of a delightful couple – he is a builder – and their young son. It was in shooting country that we visit only in March once the shooting season is over, and it is always nice to visit a fresh piece of country.

As we hacked along the lane to the first draw, a white van careered past us. A gang of twelve to fifteen saboteurs, all dressed in black and some wearing balaclavas and carrying staves, were

'Gate, please!' *by Hugh Thomson*

intent on disrupting our peaceful, law-abiding day. They intimidated children, hurling foul abuse and obscenities at them, and tried their best to provoke adults. They harassed the hounds, blew hunting horns, sprayed nasty-smelling substances, and played musical tapes of hunting in an attempt to lure them away, often towards a road, where they might be run over. They drove their vehicle over young, growing corn in order to get past the riders on the track, and when the landowner politely asked them to leave, they laughed in her face and continued. What saddened me so much was that it is these people, via the vote in the House of Commons, who now hold sway in our once-lovely country.

In April 2003, the progress of the hunting bill was temporarily suspended because of the war in Iraq. Its committee stage had been completed and its third reading was due before the Easter recess.

The original bill, which was an attempt to base some permission for hunting on 'utility and cruelty' criteria, was made tougher during the committee stage, proposing a complete ban on hare hunting, all lowland hunting, stag hunting and the digging out of foxes. In effect, it would leave only hill hunting in areas such as Cumbria.

On June 30, as this book went to press, the bill made its delayed reappearance in the House of Commons and the Government dramatically abandoned its own months of work to a backbench amendment, allowing a vote to go ahead for a complete ban. It was passed by 362 votes to 154.

Yet, as I hope shines through in this book, hunting is an apolitical activity, a civil liberty, enjoyed by people from right across the social spectrum, in rural areas all around Britain. If this bill becomes law, it will wreck a huge swathe of country life.

II From Ancient Times

For a thousand years, a mighty, gnarled, aged oak has stood like a sentinel in Savernake Forest, Wiltshire, a witness to the baying of staghounds in the past and to the tongue of foxhounds today. The ancient tree's bulging girth is held together by iron bands and lorries rumble along the road within two feet of her, but still she is just alive.

The Craven Hounds in Savernake Forest *by T. Smith*

Hunting is much older than a mere millennium. The hunting instinct is as old as man the hunter-gatherer. Ten to fifteen thousand years ago – or maybe twice that long – there were in the Americas Amerindians who arrived by land from Asia over what is now the Bering Strait and brought with them dogs that they used to hunt game.

Hunting is featured in the Bible. It was Nimrod, the son of Cush and great-grandson of Noah, no less, who was described in the Book of Genesis as 'a mighty hunter before the Lord'. He was king of Babylon around 2000 BC. The name Nimrod still means a skilful hunter or any great hunter. There is also a story that Abraham, searching for his son Ishmael, found his tent in the desert and was told by his wife that he was out hunting.

William Somervile wrote in his preface to *The Chace* (see p. 178), 'It is most certain that hunting was the exercise of the greatest heroes in antiquity. By this they formed themselves for war; and their exploits against wild beasts were a prelude to their future victories.'

The Hittites, the ancient inhabitants of Asia Minor from 1700–1200 BC, used archers in a chariot to hunt lion. In about 400 BC and 350 BC respectively, two wealthy Greek citizens, politicians and military leaders, Xenophon and Arrian, wrote about hunting with knowledge and enthusiasm. Xenophon took hunting the hare as his subject, while Arrian described the hound breeding and kennel management of gaze hounds.

In 350 BC, one Darius III, satrap (meaning viceroy, or governor) of Persia, penned his own obituary thus: 'I loved my friends, I was an excellent horseman and a brilliant huntsman.' Unfortunately, twenty years later he was killed by his own supporters.

In Roman mythology, Diana was goddess of hunting and the moon; in Greek mythology she was known as Artemis, envisaged as a virgin huntress and goddess of chastity, childbirth and the young.

HYMN TO DIANA

Dian! Hear us when we pray,
Send us foxes fleet and strong,
Grass to speed them on their way,
Hounds to hustle them along!
Hunters that can do no wrong,
Fences stout and ditches deep,
That our place among the throng
May be worth our while to keep!

By the blood of which we came,
Make us sportsmen unafraid;
Grant us that we play the game
Straightly as it should be played,
Giving place and giving aid
As a comrade may require,
Bringing pride but to be laid
On they glowing altar-fire.

Dian! Goddess of the Chase,
Ride with us across the wold,
Grant that we may take our place
With the boldest of the bold;
But if Chance her best withhold
And a fence our fate supply,
Let us, low amid the mould,
Cheer the chase as it goes by!

Will Ogilvie

The old oak in Savernake Forest

It is said, though it may be apocryphal, that the Roman general Constantius I (*c.* AD 250–306) fell asleep while out hunting near the Tiber, and in his dreams found a lovely maiden in a castle surrounded by mountains, with a pack of hounds around her. It took him three years before he found the Princess Helena in Carmarthen Castle in Wales. When she heard his story and his passion for hunting, she agreed to marry him. The couple had a son, who became Constantine the Great and the only emperor of Rome born in Britain.

In AD 642, Penda, King of Mercia, kept hounds at Pytchley, Northamptonshire, with his huntsman, Alwyne. Today's Pytchley Hunt was founded in 1750 by the 3rd Earl Spencer (Princess Diana's ancestor), and has benefited from the services of renowned huntsmen such as Charles Payne and William Goodhall in the nineteenth century, Frank Freeman and Stanley Barker in the first half of the twentieth century and, for the last three decades, Peter Jones.

As a sport, we have much to be grateful for to the Norman Conquest of 1066, when stag-hunting, already recorded in Greek mythology, became popular in the New Forest. Hounds were used to flush out the deer, and then chased by men on horseback equipped with bows and arrows – somewhat akin to the bizarre new laws in Scotland today. The New Forest, though much smaller now, still covers a beautiful tract of land in Hampshire with its ancient oaks, pretty glades and open heath and its deer and native ponies. It also has many human visitors, especially during the summer. Hunting through the forest can be fast and furious, ducking low beneath boughs, listening hard for the direction of the hounds, galloping through mud and over logs and streams. In one glade there is the Rufus Stone, erected in 1745 but commemorating the death in 1100 of William II, who was killed by an arrow.

By Tudor times every great English manor house kept a herd of deer enclosed in its parkland. Queen Elizabeth I, in 1580, kept packs of buckhounds, harthounds, harriers and otterhounds, and at the age of seventy-seven she was still hunting several times a week on horseback. In this era, foxes were killed as vermin by the peasantry. Many deer parks were destroyed in the Civil War, and hare hunting with harriers became most popular. In 1641, the Solicitor-General, Oliver St John, told the House of Lords, 'It is true that we give law to hares and deer because they are beast of chase, but it was never accounted either cruelty or foul play to knock foxes and wolves on the head as they can be found, as they are beasts of prey.'

At about this time, the sport of fox-hunting began to evolve around the great nobles' estates of Great Britain. This aristocratic image, even in today's proletarian world, is one it has never been able to shake off, yet even three and a half centuries ago many of those noblemen used to encourage their tenants and friends to hunt free of charge.

There used to be many examples of great hunting estates: the Berkeleys could hunt from their castle near the Welsh border overlooking the River Severn in Gloucestershire all the way to Charing Cross on their own land. The Marquess of Abergavenny could do so from London to Brighton; his Eridge estate is now a comparatively small tract of still lovely East Sussex land just south of Tunbridge Wells. The Earl of Yarborough (Brocklesby) owned much of Lincolnshire and likewise the Duke of Rutland (Belvoir) Leicestershire. The Watkins Williams-Wynn family (Wynnstay) controlled much of the Welsh borders in Cheshire. Much of the north of England was hunted by the Duke of Cleveland, while the Duke of Beaufort's land covered much of Gloucestershire, Wiltshire and Oxfordshire (including what are now the Heythrop and Avon Vale Hunts).

The 2nd Duke of Grafton was responsible for the Act of Parliament that resulted in the building of Westminster Bridge over the River Thames in 1748. He had complained that the ferry was too unreliable when his hounds were being transported from their kennels in Croydon, south of the river, to his estates at either Whittlebury, Northamptonshire, or Euston, Suffolk.

A Hunt in the New Forest *by Walter Tyndale, 1904*

In those days, and up until the mid-eighteenth century, any foxhunt that took place was one of slow, laborious work that went on early in the morning, hunting back to its earth the drag scent laid overnight by the fox, from where it was dug out and killed. It was a part of pest control and it wasn't until the Inclosure Acts of the eighteenth century that fox-hunting became a sport to rival that of stag-hunting. For then, with hedges and fences dividing the land, it was found the fox could become a speedy pilot leading the swells of the day across country. The outcome was always uncertain, not only for the fox, who frequently got away, but also for the followers, many of whom took numerous falls.

Hunting is a great leveller and the rabbit that digs a hole and the horse that falls into it are no respecters of whether the rider is a nobleman or a chimney sweep. One thinks of the eighteenth-century Jacobite toast to the 'little gentleman in velvet', referring to the mole that dug the molehill upon which the horse ridden by King William III of Orange stumbled. As a result of his fall, the king died.

It was not long before hunting men started to boast to each other about the prowess of their hunters, wagering bets to see whose was fastest between two points. The finishing point for these matches was often a far distant steeple, and so it is entirely due to hunting that the two great sports of point-to-pointing and steeplechasing were founded.

The end of the Napoleonic Wars saw many fit young men returning from service and taking up the chase – 'the image of war without its guilt and only five and twenty per cent of the danger', in the phrase so aptly borrowed by R. S. Surtees from the seventeenth-century poet William Somervile. It is a pastime that continues to be encouraged by the military for its ability to 'sort the men from the boys', to teach an eye for a country, to make quick, correct decisions in the heat of the moment, and to encourage leadership. Fine officers and loyal men of all ranks have been produced from the hunting field – bold, fearless, courageous and disciplined, and possessing an ability to endure hardship.

Hounds at Berkeley Castle

There is no finer place for putting their qualities to the test than Leicestershire, which became a mecca for hunters in the nineteenth century. Its pastures are criss-crossed by hedges, planted as a result of the Inclosure Acts, which make challenging fences to jump; its soil is light and well drained, making an ideal surface for galloping horses; and copses and coverts were planted throughout the county specifically for holding foxes, though benefiting many other species. Once a fox had 'gone away' from a covert, the only piece of covert next available to him was another one planted some distance away, thus guaranteeing a fast and exhilarating ride in pursuit. The swells from London bought hunting boxes in Leicestershire and would spend the winter season entertaining and hunting.

With the coming of the railways in 1860, hunting was opened up to a whole new generation of participants, for businessmen could travel for a day's sport. So subscriptions began to be paid; dealers sprang up to provide horses for this new influx; hunting rules and etiquette codes began to be laid down; and hunt committees and the Masters of Foxhounds Association were formed. Packs recognized by the MFHA have always conducted themselves according to a strict code and any rare breaches have been strictly dealt with.

Even today many steeplechasers, both famous and not so, either begin or end their careers in the hunting field, especially in Britain and Ireland. An example in 2002–2003, for instance, is at the Tedworth kennels in Wiltshire, where three ex-racehorses are being used as hunt horses: Cool Gunner, Inchcailloch and Green's van Goyen have between them won no less than thirty-five races. They share the hunting of hounds under joint Master and huntsman Rodney Ellis and his kennel huntsman Steve Adams. And back in time, when Rodney Ellis was kennel huntsman to the Old Berks for the late Colin Nash, he whipped in on Proud Tarquin, from the great Leney Princess family and winner of top-class steeplechases, including the Hennessy Gold Cup, from 1976 to 1982. 'He would see a hedge and go for it as if it was a bucket of oats,' recalls Rodney.

Many jockeys, too, have learnt their trade – and stickability – in the hunting field. In Ireland, none rides more fearlessly to hounds than Paul Carberry, often whipping in to the Ward Union Staghounds (carted stag) who have a time-honoured reputation for fast and furious riding. He does this concurrently with his professional career, and he is one of the finest horsemen–jockeys riding today.

Bob Champion, winner of the 1981 fairytale Grand National on Aldaniti, was born and bred to be a huntsman, as had an impressive seven generations of his family before him. These include his father, Bob senior, who served with the Cleveland Hunt for seventeen seasons; his Uncle Jack, who was with the Old Surrey; his Uncle Nimrod, who was with the Ledbury; and

his cousin, Bridger, who worked for a while with the Croome. Bridger became better known training point-to-pointers, but thereby maintains the hunting link, for all point-to-pointers have to qualify for their sport by hunting during the season. Bob, like other little boys before him, was not keen on ponies to begin with. He would walk out on hound exercise rather than ride, and used to help his father collect fallen stock from outlying farms. At nine, he took up riding and, thanks to a family friend, began hunting. At first he would dismount at a fence and let someone else jump the pony over, and for a while he remained nervous about jumping – until, that is, a girl at school asked him to school her pony. Fired by pride, he promptly jumped it over a gate and from that day on was hooked.

Jack Champion, when he was huntsman of the Old Surrey and Burstow

Nimrod Champion bringing hounds out of a covert

III The Shires

The Shires is the colloquial name for the Quorn, Belvoir, Cottesmore, Fernie and Pytchley Hunts, covering Leicestershire and parts of Nottinghamshire, Derbyshire, Lincolnshire and Northamptonshire, as well as Rutland. The ancient agricultural market town of Melton Mowbray is renowned to some for its tasty pork pies and Stilton cheese, but to hunting men and women it is known as a centre for hunting, for it lies at the confluence of those first three principal Shire packs.

A Meet at Kirby Gate,
the traditional venue of the Quorn opening meet, by C.B., 1901

How happy Fate's darlings (more favoured than few)
Who hunt in the Shires, and aspire to a view
Of the fastest of things with the galloping Packs –
How happy (though fewer than favoured) the Cracks!

Rancher

During the mid-nineteenth century, the various Inclosure Acts brought about the planting of tempting hedges that cried out to be jumped, and with the coming of the railways there was easier access. So Melton Mowbray became a natural headquarters for the young bloods who wanted to taste the very cream of Leicestershire hunting. It became fashionable to take hunting boxes for the season, and apart from the hunting there was tremendous social life and high society parties.

The Quorn

Hunting Grace

Praise to the Lord for a fine hunting morn,
Praise for our food and the sound of the horn,
Praise for our wine, the fences, the ditches.
Ditches which crumble, we fumble, we tumble;
Praise to the Lord for a day with the Quorn.

Courtesy of the Reverend Rex Hancock

The Quorn is world famous. Although Hugo Meynell is widely regarded as having founded it in 1753, there had been hunting in the area for half a century before that. The late Gillies Shields of Donnington wrote a delightful book, entitled *Old Tom of Tooley*, describing that period, when Tom Boothby of Tooley Park hunted what was said to be the first pack of foxhounds in England in 1698. It was fifty-five years later that he handed the pack over to his grandson-in-law, Hugo Meynell. The family lived at Quorndon Hall, from which the name Quorn is derived.

Hugo Meynell's mastership lasted forty-seven years, during which time he became the first to establish order and discipline in the hunting field, not by shouting but by good humour and example.

Since then there have been many other great names and long masterships, enhanced by the best of huntsmen, such as Tom Firr, Thomas Assheton Smith (the first Quorn Master to hunt hounds himself), George Barker and Jack Littleworth.

Thomas Assheton Smith was a great sportsman and a completely rounded, educated gentleman of the nineteenth century, with wide, far-reaching abilities in many spheres of life, business and sport, especially fox-hunting.

Thomas Assheton Smith (1776–1858) was said by his biographer to be 'a model of the British fox-hunter', being a Master for half a century and possessing 'iron nerve and constitution'; he was also considered the best rider of his day. He engaged in many successful businesses, including ship-building and slate quarrying in Caernarvonshire, maintained the family mansion at Tidworth, Hants, on the death of his father and looked after property in North Wales where his mother, a Watkin-Wynn, was born, and took an active interest in science. He was also a caring philanthropist, always willing to give sums of money for good causes, and he enjoyed sailing and cricket.

Hunting, however, remained his first love. He got an early taste of 'antis' when he was canvassing for a political seat in Nottingham. He was greeted by placards bearing slogans such as 'No Fox-hunting MP', and some protesters dressed up an effigy in red coat and a fox's brush. When he tried to speak to them, they yelled and hooted and wouldn't listen to a word. Eventually, they heard him call out, 'Gentlemen, as you refuse to hear the exposition of my political principles, at least be so kind as to listen to these few words. I will fight any man, little or big, directly I leave the hustings, and will have a round with him now for love.' This was language they understood, and though narrowly beaten by his opponent, he received cheers and no more molestations. In later years, he represented Andover and Caernarvonshire in Parliament.

Members of the Quorn in full gallop

He began hunting with the Quorn. Before taking over the horn in 1802, he was present at what is probably the most famous individual run in the hunt's three centuries, known as the Billesdon–Coplow run of 24 February 1800. It was at a time when runs were generally slow, but on this famous occasion the hounds ran at 12mph for 2 ½ hours. Assheton Smith was one of only four riders, plus the huntsman, Jack Raven, to be up at the finish, many of the leading riders of the day having fallen foul of the River Soar early on. It was a run that will only cease to interest, wrote a correspondent in the *Sporting Magazine*, 'when the grass shall grow in winter in the streets of Melton Mowbray'. It was well chronicled both in verse and colour, with poems by Beth Cox and the Revd Robert Lowth, while artist Loraine Smith, one of the few to get over the river, painted a detailed picture.

Thomas Assheton Smith was much admired during his tenure at the Quorn. When he moved on, ultimately to open up the Tedworth, which he hunted for thirty-two seasons, his place at the Quorn was taken by 'Squire' George Osbaldeston (1786–1866).

Sport was always to the forefront of Osbaldeston's life. While at Eton he was the school's top boxer and one of the best at cricket and athletics – he used to run back from Ascot races to his tutor's house – and in the holidays he rode, shot, coursed and fished. At Oxford he hunted every day the hounds were within reach. A gambler, he was in later years to lose massive sums. He had a huge zest for life, was a brilliant rider across country, including in the early steeplechases (in particular the famous Leicestershire match between two top horses, Clinker and Clasher – he won on Clasher). At the age of forty-five, he rode 200 miles in under nine hours for a wager, completing the ride in 50 x four-mile heats on a succession of thoroughbreds.

OVERLEAF: Hunt Discussions *by George Wright*

When he bought Quorndon Hall and took over the Quorn hounds, Osbaldeston already had some experience of hunting harriers and foxhounds, although his tenures were all of short duration. Nevertheless, he showed good sport, and while at the Quorn he steadfastly improved the pack of hounds. He would jump anything to stay with his hounds and could not bear 'thrusters' (hunting people who are typically at the forefront of a hunt and willing to have a go at virtually any obstacle) getting too close to him or his hounds; one rider jumped on him when he had fallen, breaking his leg so badly that he was lame for the rest of his life.

Squire Osbaldeston served two spells at the Quorn, with less success at a number of other packs in between, and then he took on the Pytchley, which was notorious for its wide drains and high bullfinch hedges. Here, incredibly, he took to hunting twice a day, morning and afternoon, with two separate packs to enable him to get round all the coverts in the hunt, so at one time he was effectively hunting eight to ten 'days' a week. It was his last, longest (at a mere seven years) and generally acclaimed as his greatest mastership.

HUNTING THE WORLD'S MOST FAMOUS PACK

Michael Farrin was a professional huntsman with the Quorn for thirty seasons until his retirement in 1998. He was spotted and nurtured by Bryan Parry – a man who could blow a hunting horn in mid-air over a fence – while out hunting with the Atherstone hounds as a young member of the Pony Club in the 1950s.

Michael was the eldest of five children brought up on the family farm near Atherstone, Warwickshire, where his father, Dick, preferred to use working horses rather than tractors. It was when hounds first came over their land that Michael saddled up his scruffy 13.2hh pony called Pat, followed them, and set the pattern for his life's career. Soon he and his next brother, Tom, were both finding themselves welcomed by the members of the Atherstone Hunt and before long, their sisters, Margaret, Jo and Cathy, were regulars too. As for the original pony, Pat, he 'carted' all of them at different times over the years.

Jo Jewell, Michael's sister, recalls, 'Both the hunt and the Pony Club were very encouraging to us, and we were contemporaries with people like Michael Ings, Malcolm and Phil Arthers and the Woodward family.'

At the age of fifteen, Michael started working in the Atherstone kennels for Captain Brian Parry, and continued with him when he moved to the North Cotswold. At nineteen, Michael was appointed as first whipper-in to the Quorn; this in itself was a prestigious step but, six short years later, with the Quorn huntsman Jack Littleworth too ill to continue, it was proposed that Michael should fill his place. This caused not a little consternation in some circles, for Michael was still only twenty-five. To be hunting the world's most famous pack of hounds, with all the added responsibility that goes with it, was a tall order. But Quorn Master, the redoubtable Ulrica Murray-Smith, and hunt secretary Jonathan Inglesent, were true believers and supported him to the hilt. Their faith was rewarded with interest. Young he may have been, but not only was Michael an excellent horseman, he also possessed all the hunting skill and political diplomacy required for the top professional job in hunting, and was able to hold his own with all ranks from royalty downwards with a smile.

For the next thirty seasons, to the understandable pride of his family and admiration from many quarters of the world, Michael showed excellent sport for a hunt that was slick and well organized. His parents, Dick and Peggy, would follow by car whenever possible and Michael was always good at reporting back to the family to describe what sort of day they had had. His two sons have continued the interest: Stephen was whipper-in to the Green Spring Valley in Maryland, USA, and long-distance lorry driver Andrew is a keen supporter of the Monmouth Hunt.

Many tributes have been paid, deservedly, to Michael, who on his retirement joined the Jockey Club in the dope-testing unit. He has hunted with Prince Charles at his side and he has shown sport for up to 300 followers but, as for many a huntsman, it is the hounds who are closest to him. One in particular, Pardon, stood out in his memory.

Michael Farrin leads the Quorn hounds home for the last time, at the end of a brilliant thirty-year career as huntsman to this top Leicestershire pack

Pardon was always going to be noticed – for good or bad – for she was, unusually, black all over, the only exception being her light brown eyebrows. Luckily, she was also an excellent foxhound. Born in 1980 by Heythrop Pixton out of Quorn Helpful (whom Michael also remembers well), she was walked as a pup by Mrs Rad Thomas, and then won the overall championship at the puppy show. But it is the hunting that counts, and Pardon soon proved herself exceptional.

'She possessed real fox sense,' Michael recalls. 'Nine times out of ten if a covert was blank she wouldn't even go in to draw it, she just stayed by me. She was unafraid to cast into the wind, and she had a wonderful voice which the others knew and they all flew to her the moment they heard her because she was always right. She was a one-off and she moved like a swallow.

She was a paragon in kennel, too, as good as gold, very easy and laid back. She never had to be scolded.'

There was a time, though, when she got Michael more than a little worried. She had returned to the home of her puppy walkers, Mr and Mrs Rad Thomas, to rear her litter after whelping. Michael was due to take the couple to a farmer's supper at 7 p.m. and at 5 they discovered Pardon was missing. The couple searched and searched in increasing agitation until Michael arrived. 'What do you mean, missing?' he asked, alarmed, and drew out his horn. For the next 1½ hours he blew and blew for his favourite, but with no response. At length, Rad Thomas returned to the house to phone the supper organizers to say they would be a bit late. And there, as he reached for the phone across an armchair, was Pardon curled up comfortably in it, sound asleep.

Because of her distinctive colour, the mounted followers got to know her too over the seven seasons that she hunted. She produced a number of litters and some of her descendants are still hunting. 'She was quite simply a brilliant hound,' Michael recalls fondly.

MELTON HUNT CLUB

The Melton Hunt Club was founded by Lance Newton of Saltby, Leicestershire, with the aim of enabling outsiders to sample the delights of hunting in the Shires, and of benefiting the principal Shire hunts of Quorn, Belvoir and Cottesmore at the same time. When Lance died, his widow, the Hon. Urkie Newton, a formidable character who regularly hunted six days a week, two each with these three packs, took over the running of the Melton Hunt Club. Today, the secretary is Sally Hudson.

Typically, at the end of the season, the three hunts are likely to receive a direct donation from the club, plus a grant for improving the country, which can include hedge-cutting and 'assistance with schemes to the mutual benefit of the hunts concerned, the farmers, and the Melton Hunt Club members'. Donations are also likely to be made to the Countryside Alliance (formerly the British Field Sports Society), to the Hunt Servants' Benefit Society and to the three hunt branches of the Pony Club.

Members may have two days hunting per season at a reduced rate with two different hunts, but in their first year of membership this may not include the Quorn.

In addition to the hunting – which draws riders from many different quarters of Britain and some from further afield – there is also a highly regarded point-to-point, the annual Melton Ride and a sponsored ride.

The point-to-point, held at Garthorpe in late May, used traditionally to bring down the curtain on the season and therefore attracted high-class runners from all over the UK, with the outcome of men's and ladies' riding championships sometimes being decided too. That mantle now belongs to the rural Torrington Farmers in Devon each June, but the Melton, on its undulating track, is still one of the most prestigious point-to-point meetings.

The Ride, held each November and rotating between the three host hunts, is about as near today to an old-fashioned point-to-point between hunters as can be. Staged over $3\frac{1}{2}$ miles of natural country, there are unlikely to be more than three or four marker flags on the entire course. Riders need to walk it, and walk it again – and probably again – for not only must they learn the way but the more canny among them will also choose their own route, ensuring that they stay the right side of the few flags. Almost invariably it is won by a 'thruster'.

The advent of team chasing in the 1970s brought with it many such people to compete in the Ride, and none deserved more to win the 2002 running than Jo Jewell.

Born and bred in the Atherstone country, she grew up hunting with her brother, Michael Farrin. Jo is a housewife and mother who doesn't ride between team-chasing seasons, when the team's captain, Mike Roberts, himself a previous winner of the Melton Ride, usually provides her with a horse. After her 2002 win, she confessed, 'I'm only just coming down to earth. There's nothing like that winning feeling, even when "aged"!'

A WELL-KEPT SECRET: THE 'MONDAY CLUB'

Mention the Shires, and one thinks of prime hunting across well-hedged permanent pasture with about 200 followers. But there is another side, a well-kept secret, which those in the know call the Monday Club. This is the nickname given by the thirty to forty Cottesmore followers who go out on a Monday, meeting on the Lincolnshire side of its country. Here, there is more arable land, resulting in heavier ground and less jumping, but for the regular band who hunt on that day, this is true foxhunting. As far as they are concerned, the hundreds who hunt on the 'fashionable' Leicestershire side of the country are welcome to it. The Monday Clubbers could be termed purists – they are able to watch the hounds at work, to lend a hand here and there and to enjoy a good hunt when it comes along. The Monday Clubbers are encouraged by joint-Master and local Lincolnshire farmer Roger Dungworth, who is now also a Master of the Scarteen in Ireland. He ensures that followers can and do play a real part in the day's sport, going off on point, helping, watching, waiting.

I was lucky enough to be part of this band for a day a few seasons ago from a meet at Martin Trollope-Bellew's farm in Barholm. The host's generosity more than lived up to his reputation, ensuring it was with an outer warmth and inner glow that we hacked off to the first draw and I cleared the first set of rails on a strange horse with a confidence I might not otherwise have felt. The field (hunting parlance for the mounted followers) included a retired policeman (he had come to hunting via mounted duty patrolling the 'antis'), huntsman Neil Coleman's wife, Philippa, hunting farmer Bill Bishop and Lincolnshire landowner Andrew Cook, as well as a number of ladies who 'go well', including Jenny Dale, Anne Eley and Sue Houghton, and, of course, the day's host, Martin Trollope-Bellew.

Before long, two of us saw a fox away from covert, waited long enough so that he was unable to turn back (in hunting parlance, to be 'headed') and holloaed. Soon the hounds were in full cry – always a stirring sound – and we enjoyed the sort of short, sharp hunt that pumps the adrenalin, especially when we crossed one of the many Lincolnshire rivers successfully (though later in the day, the whipper-in received an uncomfortable ducking). Late afternoon saw another nice run so, when home beckoned, I went with gratitude to those who had made me so welcome and felt that inner glow that good company gives all the way back.

The Earl of Lonsdale, the 'Yellow Earl', master of the Quorn from 1872–99, and twice of the Cottesmore, always had sound advice for his huntsmen

Hark hounds are in covert! One speaks, now another –
Now, silence. A whimper, a cheer – what a chorus
Of music bursts o'er us, and swells onward-borne!
How eager our hopes now (what'er lies before us)
For it's 'Huic-holler forrard – cop forrard, cop forrard!'
'Away, garn-away!' And the Horn – *there's* the Horn!

And now – what a bustle, what hard-riding hustle!
When thrusters the strong way, the cunning their long way
(The gossips the wrong way) have galloped and gone,
Perchance, the day ended, the lilt of a song may
Coax Memory's pleasure to tread an old measure –
So fill up a glass, and again *'Forrard-on!'*

Rancher

IV   The West Country

Nowhere is hunting more staunchly
defended than in the West Country,
where every other car, it seems,
displays a pro-hunting sticker.
Hunting here is part of the social
fabric of the countryside for people
from all walks of life.
Nowhere is it better illustrated that
one does not have to jump to enjoy
good hunting. Crossing the
Dartmoor or Exmoor terrain is quite
challenging enough.

The Kill *by G. L. Harrison for the* Illustrated London News, *1932*

On my first visit to Dartmoor, I was advised, 'Whatever else, make sure you don't head off on your own. Humans as well as horses have been sucked into the bog – and it can look like ordinary grass until you are on it. Or a mist may come down and enshroud you.' Luckily, I had been lent a horse by the Master – and was rewarded with one of the best hunts of my life, 7 miles at flat-out pace behind the Spooners and West Dartmoor hounds. There were only two people at the finish and any jumping would have slowed down our progress.

'WOMEN ASTRIDE? NEVER!'

In the early 1800s, the famous hunting parson Jack Russell, after whom the terrier was named, was the first person known to have hunted the Lamerton country, which then covered 400 square miles of Devon and Cornwall, including much of Dartmoor.

Born in 1795 in Dartmouth, Jack Russell was educated at Plympton Grammar, Blundells in Devon and Oxford. While at Blundells he began hunting with the staghounds. In 1819, he was offered a curacy near South Molton, and there he got together six couple of otterhounds and hunted them in the summer. The local foxhounds were already owned by another parson, the Revd John Froude. Once Jack Russell married and moved to Iddesleigh, he accumulated twelve couple of foxhounds and began hunting them. It was not an easy country, but he built up a reputation so that soon he was being invited to hunt up to 70 miles from home. He would take his hounds and stay for a week with a local landowner – meanwhile it became necessary for him to employ an understanding curate at home.

He moved away from the Lamerton in 1832, but stayed in the West Country, where his hunting prowess became legendary. At the age of seventy-nine, for instance, he hunted every day of the week from Ivybridge and on the Saturday he left at 2 p.m. to hack the 70 miles home. In later years he became a guest of the Prince of Wales at Sandringham; when the Prince went stag-hunting on Exmoor in 1879, every available coach was hired to carry people to the meet. When Jack Russell died, at the age of eighty-eight, some 1,000 people attended his funeral at Swymbridge near Barnstaple.

While the Lamerton has always remained a small, local farmers' pack, it has also always had its fair share of characters, such as farming twins William Leamon, who was Master, and Tom, his whip. They are remembered for a particular day in the 1860s from Bratton Clovelly when the first fox was killed after a 9-mile point (a 'point' being the distance in a straight line between the start and finish; in reality, hounds and followers are likely to have traversed much further). The second ran for 20 miles with just the brothers and one other there at the end; the hounds and horses were so exhausted that they did not reach the kennels until 2 a.m.

Bogs have always been a danger and during a famed run of 1889 it became impossible to follow on horseback because of them. Four riders, including a girl on a 13hh pony, were left to look after ten horses in addition to their own, while the other riders, including the Master and huntsman Henry Sperling, set off in pursuit of the hounds on foot. But then one of Dartmoor's fogs came down and it was just before dark that the group of four was rescued, though by that time four of their equine charges had escaped and had to spend the night on the moor.

Henry Sperling at one time kept and hunted both the Lamerton Harriers and Lamerton Foxhounds at his own expense, before any subscriptions were charged. He became a popular and respected man, laying on good breakfasts as well as fine sport for those who followed his hounds.

The Revd Sabine Baring Gould (1834–1924), author of 'Onward Christian Soldiers' and, less well known, the Lamerton Hunt song, said that West Country people were 'noted for their good nature and for their love of sport; they heard nothing of class hatreds' and, he added, he thought the hunt 'was a means of welding the different classes together', an observation that holds equally well today and flies in the face of popular myth.

The End of the Bye-day *by G. D. Armour, 1926*

Among the hunt followers were a baronet, Sir William Trelawney, and his attractive daughters who, in the 1890s, would think nothing of swimming their horses across the Tamar instead of making the long detour over Newbridge. There was also an elderly sporting farmer who used to hunt on a small white pony. When confronted with an ordinary-sized bank, the farmer would dismount, climb over and the pony would follow, but when faced with a big bank, the pony went first and the farmer held on to its tail to get a pull up, and the pony then waited for him on the other side.

In 1896, Henry Sperling gave his hounds to the Lamerton country and Sam Adams took on the mastership until 1904, during which time he built up a fine pack of hounds, using Four Burrow and Dartmoor blood, and for the first time they appeared in the *Foxhound Kennel Stud Book*.

In 1910, when John Cooke Hurle was Master and huntsman, the local paper reported a joint meet of the Lamerton with the Tetcott: 'Never has such a gay and animated scene been witnessed at Otterham station … special trains brought a large batch of horses … there were several motor cars, many carriages and a host of people on foot … it was a very pretty sight to see over 100 horses going at a spanking gallop over several miles of open country.'

It was at about this time that the issue of women riding astride was raging. Mrs Ethel Godfrey, Lamerton secretary for twenty-two years, was adamant she 'would never ride astride', while *The Times*, in 1914, quoted its medical correspondent: 'Woman, as the mother of the race, must on no account jeopard-ize her ability to perform the function of motherhood safely and efficiently.' Another scribe wrote in 1913:

the habit of centuries has decreed that the inferior sex shall ride side-saddle … women, for some inscrutable reason, appear to find it a very difficult matter to obtain a strong seat astride. Conformation has probably a good deal to say to it … with the majority of children and women who ride astride, this question of fixity of tenure seems likely to prove a rather serious barrier to the permanent adoption of the cross saddle.

He (I'm assuming the writer was male) added that 'much of the opposition to women riding astride was probably due to the appalling spectacle the first pioneers made of themselves … in their short, tight-fitting coats and long, flapping astride skirts.'

The First World War was looming and after that, women wearing breeches and riding astride were accepted, but it was not until after the Second World War that it became the norm. Women had, in fact, ridden astride up until the sixteenth century. Most travelled by cart or carriage, but those who rode wore long hose, just as the men did. It was during the latter half of the sixteenth century that they began riding side-saddle with specially designed clothes. Early in the seventeenth century they rode in clothes similar to everyday wear, but soon they copied men's wear of coats and waistcoats that they wore over a long skirt stiffened by layers of petticoats.

In the early 1920s, Captain Guy Babbington was Lamerton Master twice, and throughout the 1930s and the Second World War. He introduced Cricklade blood during the period when that pack was separated from the Vale of White Horse (VWH) Hunt, as well as stallion hounds from the Puckeridge Hunt. This resulted in larger hounds, and it was he who instigated the renowned West of England Hound Show at Honiton.

There could be no hunting during the Second World War as the hunt staff had been called up, but Captain Babbington kept and bred from a number of hounds to maintain the Lamerton line. Having had no more than basic exercise during the war, the hounds were fairly wild when hunting resumed. Frank Gerry, who had come to the kennels before the war, first driving the flesh cart and then as kennel huntsman and whipper-in, became huntsman after the war.

There was one particular post-war run when he was carrying the horn that is still remembered. It illustrates the hunting saying 'a three o'clock fox' – referring to the fact that when the temperature cools, the scent will improve, and if a late fox is found it can mitigate what might otherwise have been a quiet day. On this occasion, a fox jumped up at 3.20 and Frank Gerry said he would 'give him twenty minutes, then go home'. But the fox and hounds had other ideas. For the first half-hour they 'ran as fast as a point-to-point'. By then it was beginning to get dark, but on they ran, across rivers, over farms, through woods, until eventually the few remaining riders – including a lorry driver riding a tiny pony – found the hounds in an orchard surrounding a chicken run. They gave up and rode home in the dark. The next morning the chicken owner was in for a surprise: he opened the coop door and out came a very stiff fox, so tired that he had eaten only one hen!

The story of the Lamerton is typical of many hunts – including sterling efforts to keep it afloat during the two World Wars – and today, with Tony Boon, who has hunted the hounds since 1981, breeding from Pytchley, Berkeley and Tiverton lines, tradition continues. Mrs Sue Moorshead, a joint-Master since 1986, is related by marriage to Henry Sperling, Master at the end of the nineteenth century, and to the Cooke Hurles, Masters early in the twentieth – a fitting reminder of hunting's continuity in to the twenty-first century.

A FAMILY TRADITION

Nowhere is continuity better illustrated than with the Cotley, a harrier pack on the Dorset, Devon and Somerset borders that has been in the Eames family of farmers for more than 200 years. It is famed for its neat, nearly white hounds, which can be seen easily in the small fields, numerous coverts, high banks and hedges, and narrow, overgrown lanes.

The Eames family has farmed at Cotley since before the Domesday Book; it is believed a pack of hounds was run by the Palmer family, who were ancestors, for about fifty years prior to 1796. From that year, Thomas Deane hunted the hounds for some fifty-nine years, chiefly hunting hare, then, in 1836, he was faced with a huntsman's ultimate nightmare.

To those most closely connected with hunting, it is the hounds that are paramount in their eyes, with horses or one's own feet being mere tools for getting around. Years of study and thought goes into the hound breeding and every huntsman has his own individual favourites. So imagine the distress when

faced with putting down your entire pack. Yet this is what happened when rabies struck. By chance, just one bitch, Countess, was at the time in the care of Mr W. K. Eames. She became the foundation of the new pack although, in the time-honoured tradition, other hunt Masters, including several priests, rallied round by donating enough hounds for the Cotley to continue.

In the early years, mostly hare was hunted – one hunt in the 1880s from Cockcrowing Stone near Wanborough produced a three-hour hunt through five parishes – but if a fox appeared, that would be hunted too. In 1894, the story goes, after a cracking good hunt from Wotton Hill, the fox ran through the shrubberies at Broad Oak and, with the help of a rockery on the take-off side, jumped a 9-foot wall into the kitchen garden; then, by the aid of a pear tree, he got out over another wall of the same height into the fowl yard, where hounds, via an open gate, accounted for him.

Thomas Deane junior and Thomas Palmer Eames shared office in 1885, but Deane married and left the area soon afterwards. An Eames has been Master ever since, with Edward Eames holding office for forty-three years from 1886 until 1929. From the Second World War until 1965, Lieutenant Colonel R. F. P. 'Dick' Eames was joined by Captain J. Harding; the Colonel continued on until 1979, a stint of forty years, and was joined by his son Vyvyan in 1972.

It has been the tradition throughout the Cotley history for the sons of the current incumbent to act as whippers-in, and this, too, has helped in the hunt's continuity. But in the year 2000, it looked as if an outsider might have to be asked to take over, for Vyvyan suddenly announced that he could not continue. Although his son and nephew both acted as whips, they were too young and too committed to work to take over. Vyvyan's younger brother, Edward, had, of course, grown up with the family tradition but, although he hunted a little, he had concentrated mostly on the farming. His wife, Janet, a former point-to-point rider, is secretary of the hunt point-to-point meeting. Edward admitted he knew precious little about hound breeding or hunting a pack of

OVERLEAF: *Lands Well Into the Next Field by Cecil Aldin, 1932*

Colonel Dick Eames

hounds, and fifty-three years old is unusually late to start learning. However, rather than let the family tradition die, that is what he did, and he has gone into it whole-heartedly.

'I'm learning rapidly. I know the type of hounds I like and don't like, and I'm trying to breed them a bit smaller again. Obviously I know the country and many of the farmers and that's a big advantage. I'm glad that it's been able to continue on, and I hope one of our

sons, my Fred or Vyv's Tom, will be able to carry it on in the future. It's useful having Fred out; he's a member of the Young Farmers, so he knows a generation that I don't. It's important that the young know we are ordinary people who happen to like hunting.

'The foot followers are brilliant; I think hunting in this part of the world is as much to do with social services [it gives country people interaction and something to do]. There are a lot of farming supporters and two fairly large commercial shoots and they are very tolerant about hunting.

'I feel humble to be in charge, but I inherited a tidy ship. I'm lucky.'

His wife added that a ban on hunting would affect the social fabric of the countryside horrendously and social activities would fizzle out. During the 2002–2003 season Edward Eames has found the support he received phenomenal, with tremendous goodwill shown from farmers, riders and followers alike. They were all rewarded with an excellent season.

A HUNTING COLOSSUS

A colossus among hunting men in the second half of the twentieth century, Captain Ronnie Wallace almost *was* hunting: President of the Master of Foxhounds Association for twenty-two years, a great hound breeder and producer, and Master and huntsman for twenty-five seasons at the fashionable Heythrop, he had completed a further twenty-eight (21 of them carrying the horn) with the Exmoor when, in February 2002, he was killed at the age of eighty-two in a car crash on his way to visit his wife of thirty-eight years, Rosie, who was in hospital.

Ronnie Wallace grew up in the Eridge country, the woodland pack in East Sussex, where he and his two brothers began hunting. Will Freeman, brother of the legendary Frank, huntsman of the Pytchley from 1906 to 1930, was the Eridge huntsman. Ronnie liked nothing more than to follow the track down to the secluded Eridge kennels to help with hound exercise and to listen to hunting stories. It was all the incentive he needed to determine to become a huntsman himself. When, almost inevitably, he put together a 'bobbery' pack of assorted canines to hunt hares and rabbits, it was Will who gave vital advice to the schoolboy.

His parents, keen hunting people themselves, used to take the three brothers hunting on Exmoor during the summer holidays, so inspiring Ronnie's love of moorland hunting. Soon, he added summer otter hunting and following the Bolebroke Beagles and, while an Eton pupil, the Eton College Beagles to his list of interests. While Master and huntsman at Eton, his future reputation

Captain Ronnie Wallace

was founded: there were record numbers of hares accounted for, record number of days hunted, record number of followers out. These things only happen if the hunting is good and well run. Even then, Ronnie was good at visiting farmers, proficient in organizing days and unafraid of chastising errant followers. This seems to be a prerogative of amateur huntsmen, but Ronnie was sure to make amends with culprits at the end of the day.

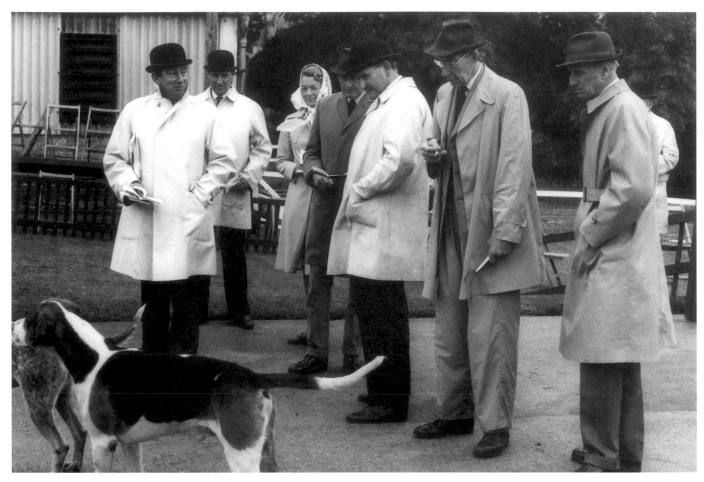

Ronnie Wallace (far left) at the Heythrop Puppy Show, 1974, with Simon Clarke, Neil Foster, Charles Barclay and Bob Field-Marsham

Ronnie led the Christ Church Beagles as an undergraduate at Oxford and his own scratch pack at Sandhurst on the outbreak of the Second World War. After the war, his first mastership was of the Ludlow pack of foxhounds. He also hunted the Hawkstone and Wye Valley Otterhounds and, for one spell, was Master of the Teme Valley concurrently with the Ludlow, a task that involved huge mileage and responsibility. A move to the Cotswold put Ronnie on view to a wider audience and he did not fail: he improved the hound breeding, increased the number of days hunting and, yet again, showed consistently good sport.

Next he moved on to the Heythrop, a pack that had previously always employed a professional huntsman, and would

again a quarter of a century later, when Ronnie moved to Exmoor. At the Heythrop, he hunted five days a week and mounted followers sometimes numbered more than 300; in other words, it soon became as fashionable to follow the Heythrop as to hunt in the Shires. It was easy to see why: sport was excellent. By the end of each season, the foxes were said to be as fit as the hounds and horses.

But it was not only the hunting of the hounds that taxed Ronnie's mind. Once again his aptitude at organization proved paramount. No matter how long the day in the saddle, Ronnie would go visiting the farmers over whose land they had hunted that same evening, while the followers who had enjoyed their day behind him could luxuriate with hot baths and glasses of whisky.

The Royal Peterborough Hound Show

The hunt staff included two full-timers who built hunt jumps in the summer and repaired them during hunting days in the winter. There was an excellent terrier man, competent kennel and stable staff, and able field-Masters who had to control the huge mounted fields and keep them in touch with but not too close to the hounds. Ronnie appreciated the quality of his kennel staff throughout his career, right from his Eton days.

In 1977, Ronnie Wallace moved on to Exmoor, the land he loved so much, where he was to remain in office until his death in 2002. He had a great respect for Dartmoor, describing it as 'an amazing place, with very tough going and where hounds run faster than they do on Exmoor, making them very difficult to live with.'

Ronnie was truly a 'hound man'. Two abiding strengths that other aspiring huntsmen would do well to follow were his quiet way of hunting hounds, only giving vocal assistance when truly needed, and his abhorrence of hitting the hounds: he would far rather his whippers-in were way out ahead on 'point' than berating the hounds, 'dog walloping' as he called it. As a result, he always had contented hounds that were happy to do their best for him. On the horn, Ronnie was superb and several times won the annual horn-blowing competition at the Horse and Hound ball.

Much of his summer months, when not hunting otterhounds, was spent attending the great hounds shows and the local hunt puppy shows (see p. 120). Ronnie Wallace graced the flags of Royal Peterborough Hound Show for half a century, winning

thirty-three championships (nineteen with Heythrop hounds and fourteen with Exmoor). Yet he always had time to help a small, less well-known hunt. Interestingly, there was one year when Ronnie had a hound, Cardinal, whose conformation was of a perfection seen only once in a lifetime. The Peterborough judges thought so too, and made him overall champion even though he was unentered, but when he began his hunting career that autumn, he simply did not take to it. Conversely, a hound who has been 'thrown out' first at the annual puppy show may be the recipient, a year later, of the 'best entered hound' award, which only goes to prove the adage ''andsome is wot 'andsome does.'

In his prowess at breeding lay part of the secret of Ronnie's success, but to complete the picture also meant hunting them superbly and organizing the country thoroughly. His enjoyment of hunting stemmed mainly from the rewards of aiding hounds to catch their fox, and of breeding the hounds capable of doing so. He will be remembered throughout hunting history.

And now Farewell. Hard ride we day by day
Yet not outstrip the ever-westering Sun.
Is it Farewell? Then fare ye well – as they
Who homed before us, all their faring done.

But, after that Farewell which all must bid
To Man and Horse and Hound – and so depart –
After Farewell, though in the shadows hid,
Can we be sure they are such leagues apart?

Yes! When the mettled pride of noon is spent,
The last long-quavering note is blown,
Turn we to face the gloaming – well content
To dread no more we must hack Home, alone.

Rancher

A Day in the Vale *by G. D. Armour, 1926*

A DAY IN THE VALE

It is a glorious winter morning in the finger of Blackmore Vale that belongs to the South Dorset Hunt; the sun shines warmly out of a cloudless sky. The knot in my stomach tightens involuntarily as we near the meet. It always does, no matter how good the horse. The teenage girl beside me, who has been chattering nervously most of the way, falls silent. It is to be her first day in the Vale, a bit like catching one's first fish, a landmark in any sporting youngster's life. It is a convivial meet. The port is good; the company mixed but all sharing one common bond – the love of hunting. Hunting in the Vale ends in late January to give this notoriously wet land a chance to recover for the spring farm work and, after a month of hunting has been missed due to a freeze-up, there is a sense of anticipation all around on this particular day.

Scotty has come down from the Borders to Dorset. He is as immaculate as always, from his anachronous topper to his cream silk gloves, riding a hireling. Beside him is the ever-smiling joint-Master, who is also the field-Master. Surreptitious good-humoured bets are taken on how many falls he will have today (four). Also among the mounted followers is the local chimney sweep, a number of current and ex-army officers, several farmers and assorted hard-riding ladies.

The amateur huntsman, who is also the senior joint-Master, arrives with the pack, sterns waving as they mill joyously around his horse's feet. They are kept together by the dependable whipper-in, he of the glorious voice; no one else holloas quite like him.

Several more mounted visitors arrive from neighboring hunts and from further afield, so soon the field numbers sixty, double its usual size. They are not to be disappointed. Wags were saying scent was bound to be bad with such bright sunshine and everywhere so unseasonably dry, but not a bit of it.

Hounds find straight away in the first covert and, not hanging about, head towards an historic nearby hill and away down the far side, pointing for notorious Brickyards, the downfall of many for decades, for buried within each blackthorn hedge are iron railings four rungs high. How the old hands love taunting newcomers with tales of past mishaps ...

A hunt on Dartmoor

But the real sport comes later in the day when, with the sun and the temperature sinking and the scent rising, we get off on a true 'three o'clock fox'. Hounds scream away, the going, unusually, is perfect and springy and, as we gallop rhythmically up to the crest of the hill, the panoramic view of the whole vale opens up: a pale, moving stream of hounds in full cry, a splash of red behind them and the black of the big, wide blackthorn hedges etched against the winter sun.

Down the hill, straight through a cover – Charlie is clearly in a hurry – past the stud and over normally wet fields we ride, taking fences in our stride, a rare treat. Down a lane, which was flooded last winter, and bearing left, we are in adjacent hunt country now and still hounds have not checked. A downhill hedge looms, blackened further by the sinking sun behind it. Some followers opt for the longer way round by a gate. God, that's tempting. Inwardly remonstrating with myself, my horse knows better and soars over – he is a natural – and as we gallop on towards the brook the adrenalin is pumping again. With this partner beneath me, we can tackle anything! Hounds check, horses with heaving flanks and sweating necks welcome the break and many riders dismount as more stragglers catch up. Every face is smiling. It has been a perfect day.

STAG-HUNTING ON EXMOOR

Stag is a Peer,
Hind is his Lady;
Haunters of the Deer
Bosky and shady –
Somerset combe, dell of fair Devon – and cool
(Friend to the hunted) swift water and shadowy pool.

Rancher

Exmoor, this most beautiful and rural tract of England, with its pretty heather, windswept trees, steep coombes and idyllic villages, is to hunting what Newmarket and its heath are to flat-racing. That its sport's very existence is threatened seems abhorrent to those who care for freedom of choice, sport, livelihood, social life … and, in particular, conservation of the deer population.

It was in the reign of Queen Elizabeth I (1558–1603) that Exmoor was hunted as a royal forest. A pack was kept at Simonsbath by the moor ranger, one Hugh Pollard, and for many years until the 1780s members of the Acland family were Masters. The nineteenth century brought a chequered spell. Although the pack became a subscription one in 1803, there were spells when the hunt was disbanded due to financial pressure. In 1825, the whole pack was sold abroad, and with that the last true staghound blood left the British shores. Subsequent packs contained mostly foxhound strains, but size has been bred back into them.

Hunting on Exmoor is about as ancient and traditional as can be found and the local strength of feeling for the sport is almost tangible, even to a summer visitor. That many of the farmers tolerate the number of red deer on their land only because of their love of hunting is indubitable. It is equally certain that were hunting banned, many of those same farmers would shoot so many deer that the ancient herds would be decimated. This is exactly what happened on Dartmoor about 200 years ago: the farmers were fed up with the deer ruining their crops, so they got rid of them, wiped them out. When hunting on Exmoor was going through difficult spells, the same thing nearly occurred; farmers culled the deer by gun, either because they were threatening their livelihoods by eating or damaging the grass and crops or because they could augment their earnings by the sale of venison.

There are two very big differences between stag-hunting and either fox- or hare-hunting. The first is that in stag-hunting, the quarry is selected in advance and then only that individual animal is hunted. The second is that foxhounds, harriers and beagles kill their quarry themselves and usually eat it; by contrast, the staghounds run their quarry to bay – just as wolves did in days of yore – but today the stag (autumn and spring) or hind (winter) is dispatched equally cleanly and swiftly, but by a gun at close range.

So, where in most forms of hunting it is the whole pack of hounds and the huntsman who are the most influential in the outcome, with stag-hunting it is the early morning work of the harbourer, who selects the deer that is oldest or weakest or otherwise most suitable for culling, and the tufters – a specially chosen, experienced small group of hounds – who turn it away from the herd, who play a crucial role. Only then is the whole pack 'laid on'. At the end of hunt, the hounds are given the offal to eat and the venison is shared among the farmers on whose land the hunt has taken place. This system has meant, over the years, that a herd of about 2,500 red deer, of which about 500 are culled annually, is maintained and thrives. It is literally the survival of the fittest, just as in the days of the wolves. As joint-Master since 1987, Mrs Diana Scott says, 'Ours is arguably the easiest form of hunting to defend; we have got such a good case because it is really herd management.'

The Devon and Somerset Staghounds are kennelled at Exford, and this village just about *is* Exmoor and hunting. In the spring, when most other packs have finished for the season, Exford becomes a mecca for hunting people. They arrive from all quarters of Britain and abroad; some bringing horses, others hiring them; some staying in the White Horse and the Crown, others choosing bed and breakfast. They can listen to the hounds singing in kennels; they can carouse with friends late into the night.

The steep and rough land of Exmoor means a sure-footed horse is more important than a jumping one, though, interestingly, most of the horses used by the hunt staff and Masters, some fifteen to twenty in the stable, are thoroughbreds, or nearly so, perhaps because joint-Masters Diana Scott and her husband Maurice have for many years run a successful competition stud. The kennels house some fifty couple of hounds looked after by huntsman Donald Summersgill since 1991 and up to eight hunt staff. The future for them in 2003 remains uncertain.

ABOVE: *Stag hunting on Exmoor*
LEFT: Haunts of the Deer *by Lionel Edwards, 1931*

V The South-East and Home Counties

The Eridge Hunt covers a beautiful piece of East Sussex just south of Tunbridge Wells, where there is much woodland and heavy clay grassland in small hill enclosures in between the woods, a contrast to the more open, wider spaces of West Sussex or of the rolling Southdowns, with which pack the Eridge amalgamated in 1981.

Fox hunters and hounds gather in Tickham, Kent, ready to commence the hunt, c. 1940

WOODLAND MUSIC

The hunt was founded in 1879 by Lord George Nevill, who kennelled the pack at Eridge Castle, seat of his father, the Marquess of Abergavenny. The family maintained its links with the hunt until the amalgamation with the Southdown just over a century later.

As a child I always heard the Eridge described as a 'good country for children to start in and for older riders to retire to'. Certainly I found it a good place to begin hunting: there was always something happening with a certain amount of challenge but nothing to overawe a child. It also earned a deserved reputation for nurturing future top-class professional huntsmen. The way hunting has been able to continue in the crowded yet beautiful South-East and Home Counties has been through several hunt amalgamations: the Tickham and the West Street; the Old Surrey and Burstow and the West Kent; the Romney Marsh and the East Sussex; the Chiddingfold and Leconfield with the Cowdray, the Enfield Chace and Cambridgeshire. For the 2002–2003 season, the Garth and South Berks has amalgamated with the Vale of Aylesbury, itself a merger in 1970 of the Hertfordshire, the Old Berkeley and the South Oxfordshire Hunts.

My earliest memories with the Eridge begin at the age of ten on a riding school pony led by Angela Peate (later Pelly). We would be trotting along the woodland tracks behind everyone else when suddenly there would be an about turn and we would find ourselves at the head of the field. There was much twisting

Bob Field-Marsham with Anne Holland (left) and her sister as children

and turning of the plentiful foxes in those woodlands, especially in Bayham, so desecrated in the big storm of 1987, on the Kent and East Sussex border.

There is nothing like the cry of hounds' music in woodland: it resonates and magnifies and is one of the most spine-tingling sounds on earth. One cannot often see much of the hounds in woodland, although the Eridge hounds had a lot of white bred into them to help see them against the dark woods, but one can hear them. In woods as big as Bayham, it is wise to keep close to the sound, for otherwise it is all too easy to become lost.

There were two certainties about a wood this size: there would be dozens of foxes and you would stay in the woods all day. One could add a third: ladies' hairnets were certain to be left on branches as we ducked and dived through the rhododendrons and under the whippy silver birch and thorn branches. Occasionally we would come out on the bit of grassland by the ruins of Bayham Abbey, but only to pop straight back into more woods on the other side. There were several long, straight, still partially cobbled, rhododendron-lined carriage drives from the various lodge gates that led to the 'new' abbey, built for the Marquis Camden. Nowadays it consists of rather upmarket apartments overlooking the magnificent lake.

White Hill was my favourite piece of the Eridge country, part of Eridge Park (as the Castle is known nowadays), home of the Marquess of Abergavenny. It was not nearly so dense as Bayham and its southern banks were more heathlike, full of bracken and a few silver birch trees, with fallen ones making nice little logs to jump. This swept down to the string of lakes and one lovely old house lived in by hunting stalwart, amateur whipper-in, keen beagler and local schoolteacher Rachel Crutch, who thought nothing of walking the mile uphill to the road (at least it was downhill when carrying shopping). The northern side of White Hill was dense with rhododendrons to a clearing where the hunt kennels, huntsman's house and whip's cottage were hidden away with no neighbours to disturb with baying hounds or the smell of flesh. Occasionally local foxes were caught out, so used to the sound of hounds were they.

And here's to the Provinces – provident places
Where scores of good fellows with cross-country faces
Must needs solve the problem of hunting the fox
Without three blood horses sent on in a Box.

Where the slowest of hunts may be breathless as Fate
To those who have eyes, and the instinct innate;
And the happiest memory of any may be
Of a May fox away from a gorse by the sea.

Here the heart a thought old (if it's in the right place)
Need seldom despair of outwitting the pace,
For there's riding to hunt – and there's hunting to fall –
('What – is it unjumpable? Get off and – crawl!').

Hunt at your ease, where there's seldom a crowd,
Go where you please (though a lot of it's ploughed),
You may read as you run – you may watchfully learn
If a fox runs a gateway he's done to a turn.

You may gain that which never was bought with fine gold,
In health, fun and happiness, mellow – grow old;
If they race (and they can!) be contented to prate
On the days when you too could ride just on twelve-eight.

And if some of the best – be they men, hounds, or nags –
Might be wasting their time on the tan or the flags,
Who rides once behind them may lastingly note
That a deal can't be told by the cut of a coat.

Rancher

My abiding memory of starting with the Eridge is of Major Bob Field-Marsham, one of hunting's greats. When I started, he was hunting hounds, though the wear and tear that his back took trying to support his tall, angular frame was to prove too much soon after. He was imbued with a voice to match his character:

rich, fruity, full of humour and clear as a bell. 'I want to come back in the next life as a stallion foxhound,' he used to say. 'I can't imagine a better way of living,' and his face would crease up in smiles and his eyes sparkled.

Bob F-M, as he was invariably known, was a joint-Master and huntsman of the Bicester from 1936 until 1942, then, after war service, he was appointed Master and huntsman to the Eridge in 1947, where he remained in office until 1961. During that time he built up an excellent pack of hounds and earned a fine reputation as huntsman. He shared the mastership with the Marchioness of Abergavenny.

My father, Rex, used to recount the tale of the time the Eridge met the rare obstacle, for them, of a wide ditch across the middle of a field. 'Don't worry!' called Father, 'my mare is Irish', and he set off at the gallop towards it. But Irish horses approach ditches from a trot, or less, and so she stopped; Father sailed over her head and then looked up from the bottom of the ditch as the horse popped over …

On another occasion, his horse hit a gate so hard that Father's hat was propelled firmly on to the bridge of his nose.

'Is it broken?' Lady Abergavenny, the Master, enquired.

'I don't think so,' replied Father, rubbing his nose, 'but it does hurt.'

Lady Abergavenny responded, 'I meant the gate!'

There is a tradition in many hunts that anyone who breaks a gate pays for a new replacement; if the broken one was old and rickety, a new one was the least a farmer could expect, a small compensation for allowing the riders across his land.

Towns, Railways, Motorways – and Still Hunting

'Not once in forty-four years' service with the West Kent have I woken up in the morning and thought "I don't want to go to work today".' So said Stan Luckhurst on his retirement in 1999, an ever-buoyant man and friend to many in the hunting world. It is a typical remark from a man utterly immersed in the hunting way of life. It may be glamorous to hunt a fine pack of hounds in smart uniform and be fêted by many, but huntsmen

are also the men who have to shoot day-old calves because of problems in the farming industry, or dispatch a friend's favourite hunter, or put down a faithful hound … The hours are long and manual and take place in all weathers, but there is a community spirit to hunting, and for many in the countryside it supplies all the social life, too.

Born the son of a wagoner in the Ashford Valley country, also in Kent, Stan Luckhurst always loved horses. Stan went straight into service with the Ashford Valley after leaving school in 1949, and then was called up for National Service in 1952, serving with the Horse Artillery. From there he went as kennelman to the West Kent and stayed for forty-four years. He was promoted to first whip and stud groom, then kennel huntsman to Colonel Auriol Gaselee. Colonel Gaselee, late father of Lambourn National Hunt trainer Nick Gaselee, taught Stan much about

hunting and enjoyed many humorous moments with him too. Stan was allowed to hunt hounds a few times, and the occasions were fairly predictable – usually after the Colonel had enjoyed rather a good dinner.

In 1967, Stan Luckhurst was promoted to huntsman and 'always had very good and supportive Masters', as well as first-class horses, throughout his long and distinguished career with the pack whose northern borders edge up through the Greater London suburbs to the River Thames. As with most huntsmen, it was the hounds that were foremost in his life, his pride and joy; looking at hounds in kennel before his retirement, it was self-evident that the hounds felt the same about him. He used to help laypeople get to know the hounds, too, for one of his traditions was to walk hounds out for an hour every mid-morning, accompanied by several young children and various adults. This would be in addition to their normal pre-breakfast exercise. He had a few particular favourites in his life, notably Linkman, who hunted until he was fifteen years old (exceptionally old for a hound), Decoy and, later on, Landlord, who was able to hunt 'brilliantly' with a plate in his hind leg after he was hit by a car.

When Stan Luckhurst began with the West Kent, he and Colonel Gaselee would leave the kennels – then at Plaxtol, close to Peter Cazalet's Fairlawne racing stables of Devon Loch fame – at 3.30 a.m., to hack two hours to a cubhunting meet. How times have changed. Such a hack would not be possible now – the intervening years having seen the building of the M25, M20, M26 and M2, two electric railways, including Eurostar, and housing development across much of the West Kent Hunt country. Amalgamation for the pack, founded by John Warde of Squerries in 1776, was the inevitable result, the only surprise being, perhaps, that it didn't happen sooner.

The East Kent is typical of a hunt enduring and surviving pressure. It is tucked away as far south and east as possible, in an

Stan Luckhurst in the ring at Peterborough after winning the bitch championship in 1973

Stan Luckhurst hunting with the West Kent

area that has a propensity for snow and is criss-crossed by motor-ways and railways heading for the Channel ports of Folkestone and Dover from London. It will never be fine hunting country, for it is 'cold scenting' with plenty of plough; it also has much wire, but its followers are capable of jumping it along with the best. In the most British of traditions, they make the best of what they have got and enjoy it. They are assisted by the services of a huntsman, Richard Blakeney, who since 1976 has been hunting the mainly South-East-bred hounds (using West Kent, Old Berks, and Crawley and Horsham blood, along with Heythrop and some bitches brought in from the North Cotswold).

The East Kent's reputation for the longevity of its Masters has doubtless helped it survive. The pack's first recorded Master in 1814, Sir Hugh Oxenden, most unusually, kept only spayed bitches during his fourteen years in office. One of the earliest long-serving Masters, for thirty-eight years (1832–70), was Frederick Brockman of Beachborough. He was followed by the munificent 7th Earl of Guildford who spent some £30,000 between 1870 and 1879 on rebuilding stables and kennels at Waldershare Park.

By the time H. W. Selby Lowndes came to the East Kent from the Bilsdale in 1900 at the start of what was to be a tenure spanning three decades, the East Kent Hunt was in its heyday. There were no electrified railways and no motorways, resulting in long hunts across the Vale of Ashford. In 1922, Mr Selby Lowndes proudly boasted that the great reputation which the East Kent had achieved 'is perhaps as good evidence as can be found of the vitality of the sport of fox-hunting anywhere in this country.' In those days, the hunt could easily accommodate four days' hunting per week. Today, it hunts twice a week.

In the twentieth century, Reg Older spanned three decades as Master, initially joining point-to-point rider Stuart Jeanes, and later joined by Ted Maylam and Bill Piper. Today, the Masters are Nigel Fisher and David Potter, with Richard Blakeney still going strong in the kennels. Richard can remember when a third of the marsh area of the country was all down to grass, fenced with oak rails. In those days, more than thirty years ago,

it was quite normal to jump thirty to forty sets of rails in a day. Although there is not as much jumping as that today, this resilient hunt, in a difficult country, keeps going apace.

The Happy Hunt – and Huntsman

Bob Collins is someone for whom life is either 'wonderful' or 'not a problem'. For the last twelve years he has been professional huntsman to the Hampshire Hunt, a heavily shot part of Hampshire within close reach of London, 'But,' he says, 'hunting and shooting liaise to make both sports a success, so it's not a problem.'

He has also, he says, always been blessed with wonderful Masters wherever he has been. Not surprisingly, this warmth of personality has stood him in good stead throughout his distinguished career. His childhood hero was Jim Bailey, for thirty years huntsman to the Taunton Vale where Bob grew up. Bob's grounding came under famed huntsmen and Masters such as Willie Poole (also known for his humorous writing on hunting and country life), Stephen Lambert and Nigel Peel.

Bob hunted the Curre hounds for 'four wonderful seasons'. The Curre is a small hunt just across the River Severn from Bristol, domain of great show-jumper David Broome, who was a Curre Master for many seasons. It is steeped in history and only became a subscription pack in 1952 on the death of Lady Curre. It is believed Welsh hounds hunted in the area during the 1600s and in the 1780s the pack was referred to by John Curre as the Chepstow Hunt. Like many others, the hunt changed its quarry from hare to fox in about 1820, when it was called the Blue Hunt. The first time a Mr Curre is recorded as hunting the hounds is in 1854, and by 1896 they were hunted by Mr (later Sir) Edward Curre. Edward Curre was a fine hound breeder and it is to him that the renown of the pack is owed; he ran the hunt at his own expense for thirty-four seasons until his death in 1930, when his widow, Lady Augusta, took over. In fact, until her death in 1956, the hunt was known as Lady Curre's.

Bob described the Curre Hunt country as 'wild and woolly with wonderful little white hounds'. It was there that Bob had

Bob Collins – the 'happy huntsman' for whom life is 'wonderful'

the horse of his life, called Albert. Once he measured a hedge they had jumped. It stood 6ft 3in high.

It had to be something special to lure Bob Collins away, and in 1991 he found it in the HH – Hampshire Hunt or, as it is colloquially known, the Happy Hunt. The HH has a distinctive hunt button adorned by the Prince of Wales' crest, stemming from when the future King George IV kept a pack of hounds in the area; he gave permission for the crest to be used, and each succeeding Prince of Wales has renewed the privilege. The HH was founded in about 1745 and was at one time known as the Kilmiston Hunt and, in 1784, as the Gentlemen of Hampshire Hunt. Bob Collins has melded with the HH, and is a fine ambassador for hunting further afield, too.

His funniest hunting memory, however, belongs to the Chiddingfold, Leconfield and Cowdray in West Sussex when he was kennel huntsman and first whip to Nigel Peel. It was Christmas Eve and one of the followers was Guy Harwood, the famous racehorse trainer whose first love is hunting. It was agreed that, being Christmas, they would make a short day and go home early for the sake of the staff and families. But just before 3 p.m., Nigel Peel was persuaded to have one more draw. Hounds found quickly and flew, long and hard, until, in the gathering darkness, Guy Harwood and Bob jumped 'a massive hedge off the road on to somebody's lawn where hounds were marking'. Four people crammed into a three-wheeled Robin Reliant to go and fetch the lorries, but when they got there, the hunt lorry had broken down. By the time Bob got back to where he had left hounds and Masters, the place was deserted. Eventually he found them at Guy Harwood's, horses and hounds in assorted stables normally occupied by high-class flat horses, the humans in the house downing tumblers of whisky. 'Then they decided to cut the Christmas cake,' Bob recalls with a chuckle. The various wives were not too pleased when their menfolk eventually arrived home.

THE VOICE OF HUNTING

A true gentleman of many parts, Dorian Williams was as fine an ambassador for hunting as it is possible to be. Educated, articulate and erudite, he was a good amateur Shakespearian actor, a first-class writer, an excellent show-jumping commentator, and a fine horseman.

His superb, mellifluous commentaries made him to show-jumping audiences what Sir Peter O'Sullevan was to racing fans: The Voice. But people from a different world knew him equally well as the founder, first, of the Pendley Shakespeare Centre and then, also at his family home in Buckinghamshire, of Pendley Adult Education Centre. He was also headmaster of a prep school, author of many books, a local politician, and chairman of the British Horse Society.

But, like another great 'all-rounder', Assheton Smith (see pp. 34–5), his passion was foxhunting, and in his busy life Dorian Williams knew how fortunate he was to have Albert Buckle as his professional huntsman with the Whaddon Chase (before it amalgamated with the Bicester and Warden Hill).

Hunting became Dorian's passion as a young boy living in the heyday of the Grafton country in Northamptonshire shortly after the First World War. He grew up in the ambience of a hunting home, but, aged about twelve years old, it was his first time out unaccompanied, from a Boxing Day meet at Towcester, which inspired him – an occasion he related in his autobiography, *Master of One*.

By mid afternoon that day more and more people were going home, but Dorian was determined to stay out with his faithful

Albert Buckle with his master from 1954, Dorian Williams, at Whaddon Chase, 1980

pony, Freckles, to the very end. He realized the hunting could not have been all that fast or he would not have kept up, but nevertheless hounds just kept running, hour after hour, with Freckles clearing all the fences that came his way, along with the best.

Eventually dusk fell, he had no idea where he was, and he didn't want to admit the depths of his fatigue. Finally, on the edge of Northampton and many miles from home, huntsman Will Freeman was about to give the fox best, when he spotted some crows flying low over a nearby field. Will immediately 'lifted' the hounds to the spot, they picked up the line, and within five minutes had accounted for their quarry.

'It's the crows what killed 'im,' Freeman repeated over and over again to anyone who would listen.

That night, having been found eventually by his anxious mother, who had scoured the countryside in her car with a groom looking for him, the young Dorian regaled the adventures of the day, ending, 'It's the crows what killed 'im,' a phrase which became perpetuated in family parlance.

In the 1920s and '30s, acknowledged as the heyday of hunting, the tiny Northamptonshire village of Greens Norton would see no less than 300 hunters a day out being exercised.

Dorian's father, Col V. D. S. Williams, who was twice wounded serving in the First World War, was Master of the Grafton from 1928–31 and he was an inspiration for meticulous organization, much as was seen in later decades by Ronnie Wallace (see pp. 51–4). He believed it was a basic necessity for good sport and devoted as much time to organizing a day's hunting with the Grafton as would a tycoon to his businesses, as was testified by copious entries in diaries, notebooks and accounts recording the number of hounds out, coverts drawn, foxes seen and whether killed, the horses ridden by the hunt staff. Farmers that had been upset and any damage to land or fences were all recorded, too.

It was a visit to the Williams' home that brought about the birth of the Pony Club. The visitor, Harry Faudel-Phillips, found the three Williams children, Barbara, Dorian and Maurice, immersed in the 'Tailwaggers Club' page of the daily paper. Better than that, he declared, would be to found a pony club – and from that chance remark the Pony Club was born. Even today, the name of nearly every branch is derived from and attached to its local hunt. In 1929 there were three founding branches, the Crawley and Horsham, the Shropshire, and the Grafton; in 1931 there were 59 branches totally 4,500 members and by 1934 there were 100 branches, with 8,500 members. The biggest youth organization in the world, there are today 357 branches and 32,000 members in the UK, with a further 137,000 members in 16 countries worldwide.

Only a few years later, Dorian remembered the shock of his father retiring as Master and the realization, in later years, that snobbery, or class distinction, may have come into it. The Williams were an upper-class family but not nobility. All the adjacent packs had Lords as Masters, and the Grafton, it seems, wanted one, too, appointing Lord Hillingdon.

Thankfully, times have changed, and while there are, quite rightly, still Lords and Dukes holding Masterships, there are also Masters from all walks of life and backgrounds today, including many who in yesteryear would have been deemed 'working class'. How unfortunate that the 'toff' image of hunting has outlived reality by half a century. Today, it is simply the love of the sport and the desire and time to devote to it that is important. Blue-blood breeding is the preserve, instead, of the hounds.

Dorian told another gem in *Master of One*. He was wearing old clothes to mow the grass at Pendley, his beloved Buckinghamshire home. The task was a useful keep-fit summer exercise, for the lawns took five and a half hours to mow, which necessitated him walking eighteen miles. Pendley had become a great success story with some three to four thousand people attending dozens of different courses each year. Many visitors were surprised that the Dorian Williams of television show-jumping commentary fame was one and the same person as the founder and hands-on director of Pendley. On this occasion, Dorian finished the mowing and came into the baronial hall to take tea with the guests. Naturally he was still in his working clothes.

'How nice,' remarked one guest, 'that the gardener should be permitted to come in … but why not? You've been working as hard as we have, though your work is physical, whereas ours is mental.' Whereupon he tipped him half-a-crown (12 $\frac{1}{2}$ p) – and Dorian pocketed it! Humour, and tact, were never far away in his life.

Dorian Williams became a Master of the Grafton from 1951–4, but it was at the Whaddon Chase that he will always be remem-bered. There, he forged a tremendous rapport with farmers and subscribers alike and, in particular, with his huntsman, Albert Buckle, one of the sport's finest ambassadors. For more than twenty years the two of them epitomized all that is good about hunting.

BOXING DAY

Boxing Day equals tradition: the meet in the town centre or market square; everyone dressed their very best, boots shining, jackets newly cleaned; horses turned out immaculately, tinsel plaited into their manes; the occasional sprig of mistletoe sported in a lady's lapel. It is the day the hunt 'shows the flag' to the townspeople. Often, in return, the mayor dispenses the stirrup cup. Then it is off for a jolly, a means of settling the Christmas pud and the over-imbibing of the best port.

It is the day, too, for giving the hunt staff their Christmas boxes. The cap taken from both mounted visitors and those on foot will go to them. Some riders will discreetly stuff some notes into the whip's pocket. Other hunt members will already have visited the hunt kennels ahead of the day to present their gift in person. In this way, it is not only the huntsman and whipper-in who are remembered, but also the kennelman, the groom and any other ancillary staff who fill the hard-working, unglam-orous role of 'backroom boys'.

When I was little, the Eridge used to hold its Boxing Day meet (known as St Stephen's in Ireland) on Tunbridge Wells Common, close to the rocky outcrops that have been a source of adventure for children from time immemorial. It was an excel-lent venue, with plenty of room for everyone, and people flocked in their hundreds from every direction, happy to witness the traditional Christmas scene. Family legend has it that when my brother was first taken, as a toddler, he agreed that, yes, the horses were lovely, the hounds were friendly, there were lots of smart people. 'But,' he asked, 'where's the fox?'

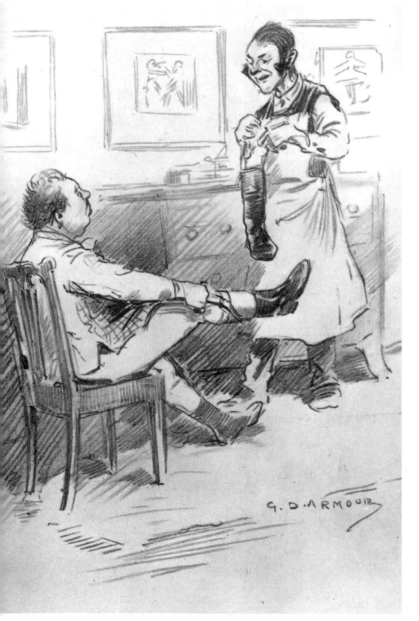

LEFT: The New Boots *by G. D. Armour, 1926*
RIGHT: The Meet at the Cat and Custard Pot *by the Earl of Ypres*

VI   The East

There was a time when the Berkeley family could hunt from their castle in Gloucestershire by the banks of the River Severn right up to Berkeley Square, in central London, entirely on their own land.

Preparing for the Chase *drawn by R. Pollard,*
engraved by F. Juke and R. Pollard

FROM BANK TO PLOUGH

It is said that as long ago as the fourteenth century the then Lord Berkeley hunted from a village called Charing, now Charing Cross railway station. Then, in some family feud, a branch of the family renamed itself Barclay and over the centuries has hunted a swathe covering most of the eastern side of England, while the Berkeley Hunt continues in the west, covering much of Gloucestershire in the area of Berkeley Castle and the River Severn, and is renowned for the big dykes or rhines that have to be negotiated.

Edward Exton Barclay was supposed, in the 1880s, to work in the family bank of that name, but he preferred hunting and farming. He took over a pack of harriers just outside Roydon, north London, from where he would put the hounds on to a train at Tottenham station and set off for the day's sport. In 1896, he moved to Brent Pelham Estate, near Bishop's Stortford in Hertfordshire, close to the Essex border. There he took on the Puckeridge hounds, and spawned four generations of huntsmen. The Puckeridge lies in the heavy plough and arable land of East Anglia and is therefore not renowned as a jumping country, but it produces excellent sport, mostly with Old English hounds.

After Edward came Maurice, known as Mo, who served the perfect apprenticeship under Frank Freeman, one of the greatest professional huntsmen of all time, while he was studying farming in the Pytchley country in Northamptonshire. In August 1914, Mo and twenty-two of the hunt horses enlisted with the Norfolk Yeomanry and saw service in France and Palestine with the British Expeditionary Force. Mo's coveted hunting horn came in useful on one occasion when he blew it to call back the water camels that had wandered away. At the end of the war, Mo returned to Brent Pelham with his well-bred charger and the donkey that had been the Yeomanry's mascot, and there they stayed for an incredible seventeen years until, in 1935, both animals died.

Mo's most memorable hunt, in 1938, lasted nearly 2 $^{1}/_{2}$ hours with a 5 $^{1}/_{2}$-mile point; it had begun fast and then became one of perseverance, and only three members of the field were there at the finish. They had run through woods, smaller coverts and deep plough, and across streams and ditches.

Mo maintained the policy of breeding pure-bred English foxhounds and it must have been hard to bear, one short year later, to put down almost all the pack's dog hounds on the outbreak of the Second World War. Most packs found

Three generations of the Barclay family, in 1947:
Edward, Maurice and Charles

themselves in a similar invidious position. There was no knowing when the war might end or when hunting would be able to resume normally. Many were kept going on a depleted, shoestring basis often by women, or else by men who were too old or too young to serve. Food, as well as staff, was in short supply. The future was too uncertain to breed more hounds, so many were put down.

It will be the same but worse should a law be enacted to ban hunting; without any prospect of a future to look forward to, many thousands of hounds – in the region of 20,000 – will have to be put down. They are pack animals, born and bred to hunt, and only a minority would make pets. Some could go abroad, perhaps a few hundred, and it would have to be hoped that some key hounds of historic packs would remain. The thought of centuries of careful and meticulous breeding being wiped out is abhorrent.

'YONDER HE GOES!'

Always our fathers were hunters, lords of the pitiless spear,
Chasing in English woodlands the wild white ox and the deer,
Feeling the edge of their knife-blades, trying the pull of their bows,
At a sudden foot in the forest thrilling to 'Yonder he goes!'

Not for the lust of killing, not for the places of pride,
Not for the hate of the hunted we English saddle and ride,
But because in the gift of our fathers the blood in our veins that flows
Must answer for ever and ever the challenge of 'Yonder he goes!'

Will Ogilvie

During the Second World War, there was one occasion when the remaining hounds were hunted by Mo's son Charlie, who was home on leave. He had only hunted beagles and harriers, before but his first with foxhounds proved memorable, with an excellent hunt. So it was not surprising that, in 1947, he joined his father, Mo, and grandfather, Edward, who died later that year, in the Puckeridge mastership.

Charles Barclay whipped in to Ronnie Wallace – perhaps the most famous twentieth-century foxhunter of all (see pp. 51–4) – at Eton, and in later life the two went on to judge at the Beaufort Puppy Show for thirty-five years. Charles hunted the Puckeridge until 1985 and remained a joint-Master until his death in July 2002, a total of fifty-five years in office, by which time all four of his children had been Masters, as well as his late wife, Laura. Sons Ted and Robert are former Puckeridge Masters, daughter Diana Pyper still is, and youngest son, James, is a former Master of the Cottesmore and Master and huntsman of the South Wold in Lincolnshire.

Growing up at Brent Pelham was, says James, a wonderful experience, not only for the hunting but also for the farming and country way of life. 'We had the most loyal farm and hunt staff, gardeners and so on. Many of them worked for the family for more than fifty years; and they always knew they could come to my father for good counsel, and they always had a cottage for life. I remember one worker who was deaf and dumb who used to live for Father's cows; he was a super fellow. Then there was Dick Bull, the kennelman, and Mabel who worked in the house; they were from a family of eleven, nine of whom worked for our family.

'The pub, the Black Horse, played a key role, where Father, the vicar and the staff all used to get together. My great-grandfather tried to buy it to close it down because he didn't approve, but luckily he failed. All the locals would congregate there for a drink after church, but on the stroke of two they would all disappear for their Sunday lunches. There was a terrier who always knew the exact time.'

There has remained a strong rapport between the Barclay family and those who live on the estate, in evidence when James and his new bride, Lucy, called to have tea with four brothers. The couple were touched to be presented with a silver tea service.

James Barclay, Diana Pyper, Charles Barclay, Ted Barclay and Roger Barclay

Part of this traditional country life was the pack of hounds, of which James says, 'My great-grandfather and grandfather, as well as my father, were well known for their hound breeding and bred a very, very good pack. They were not only good on the plough, essential for their country, but they could prove their worth when visiting other countries as well, such as the Heythrop, Warwickshire and Cottesmore.' Hounds that had influence on the pack were Duster 1915, Gleaner 1915, Ruler 1909 and Render 1913. Some years later there were Plymouth and Plunder, 1948, and Poetry, who won the Peterborough Championship in 1951.

As a small boy, James, encouraged by his mother, Laura, put together a pack of rabbit hounds that included corgis and dachshunds among the assortment. They even had their puppy show, encouraged by the Duke of Beaufort. James recalls, 'My first visit to Badminton House and staying with "Master" was in 1967; he virtually adopted my grandfather and was wonderful to us. When I took on my first pack of foxhounds, the Essex and Suffolk in 1983, he gave me a champion bitch from Peterborough to help me get started.'

Before that, James had gained both farming and hunting experience in the Blackmore and Sparkford Vale,

Warwickshire, Heythrop and North Tipperary countries and it is doubtless due to this that he learned the value of public relations with both farmers and neighbourhood, something for which he has become well known.

Next, James took on the Fitzwilliam where, in twelve seasons, he opened up some of the fens and created the old Burghley country from Lord Exeter, bringing the hunt up from two to three days' hunting per week. During this rewarding period, he saw many more people taking an interest in and following the hounds. For good measure, he also founded the Granta Harriers with some farming friends, a draft pack that hunted the fens on alternate weeks.

When a vacancy for a Cottesmore Master came up, James took the opportunity of running a totally different type of hunt and had three 'thoroughly enjoyable' seasons there, not carrying the horn and more often than not following on his feet. He played a crucial part in liaising with farmers. Then tragedy struck.

James's wife, Lucy, whom he met while at the Essex and Suffolk, was exercising her horse barely 100 yards from home when a car ran into the back of them. Lucy's spine was broken and she was paralysed from mid-back down. James speaks of her with the greatest admiration and affection. 'With guts and determination, plus help from the spinal team at Sheffield, she took part in the spinal unit games at Glasgow only fourteen months after the accident, coming fourth in the swimming – and the other three had legs that work! She was third in the shooting and she hopes to get up to national or Olympic level.'

The couple's troubles were not yet over, for, when applying to adapt their home to make it suitable for her wheelchair use, they came up against planners who treated them with, at best, disdain, and refused their plans outright. Rather than become embroiled in a demeaning fight, the couple moved on to the South Wold Hunt in Lincolnshire, where James took up the horn again and they were able to convert a farmhouse for Lucy. It is a lovely, unspoilt part of the world. 'It is probably one of the most beautiful and rural countries left in hunting today,' said James. 'There are very few visitors as they mostly whiz by on the A1. The pace of life is definitely slower.'

He drove me to a lofty spot on top of the Wolds, near where the Opening Meet was held in November; we could see the Norfolk coast 10 miles distant one way, the Yorkshire coast in another direction and turning 180°, Lincoln Cathedral, in another. James was looking forward immensely to hunting the hounds here, and to continuing his PR work for Hunting for the Community, which includes visiting inner city schools. 'The key thing hunting people must do,' he said, 'is educate the general public, to explain why hunting means so much to us in the country, what it is, how and why we do it.' Unfortunately, shortly before Christmas 2002, James, aged forty-three, suffered a heart attack. He has now relinquished the South Wold mastership but, in a bid to rebuild his fitness and to encourage local youngsters, he is forming a private pack of beagles and hopes that in time he may hunt a mounted pack of hounds again.

THE COTTENHAM CONNECTION

The late Betty Gingell was the renowned Master and huntsman of the Cambridgeshire Harriers for more than half a century from 1942. In the harrier world she had no superior, and when she died in 1995, the hunt, which originated in 1745, disbanded. A robust woman, she bred and produced hounds, as well as horses, not only to win at the Peterborough Show (the pinnacle for show hunters and hounds) but also to do the work for which they were bred in the hunting field. She was also a renowned judge. All these interests were bound together by one tie: the love of hunting.

Born in Essex, she married Cambridgeshire farmer Hugh Gingell. When they bought the land containing the point-to-point course at Cottenham, near Cambridge, in 1962, they covenanted that it should remain a point-to-point course in perpetuity. The land has never been ploughed, and raises the curtain each January on the English point-to-pointing scene. It had been established as a point-to-point course in the 1880s and throughout its history it has had a strong influence on Cambridge undergraduates, many of whom, lured by a local day out at the hunt races, have gone on to make names for themselves in the National Hunt racing world.

Betty Gingell and the Cambridge Harriers

In 1884, the course was described by undergraduates as, 'no cocktail affair or make believe, it was as good a course of hunter fences as you could find anywhere in England and they must be either jumped or let alone.' By 1899, the Cambridge University United Hunts Club was flourishing, and the club still holds an annual point-to-point at Cottenham. In those days, the organizers had to pay twelve dozen bottles of whisky to a Mr Cash, who owned three-quarters of the course and the town crier collected the gate money. In addition, two dozen Cambridge policemen were hired for 12 shillings a dozen to keep law and order. But they couldn't always keep up with welshing bookmakers who used to make their getaway through the trees at the back of the course.

The course underwent a facelift in 1924 when much of it was reconstructed and the present day grandstand was built. A racecard of that year cost 6d (2 $^1/_2$p), when the occasion was entitled the Cambridgeshire Steeplechases and Hurdle Races, run under National Hunt Rules for amateur riders, but by the next year it was back to the title Cambridge University Steeplechases.

Betty Gingell rode just once in a point-to-point. That was during the Second World War on a skewbald mare called Sally, and she finished second. But the Gingell racing colours continued to be worn first by their son Michael and currently by their grandson Matthew. Betty's husband, Hugh, also won several hunt races, notably with Cox's Orange. Horses were ridden for them by Alan Lillingstone, who has lived and hunted in Ireland for many years, and Ian Balding, recently retired as a flat trainer but still a great man riding to hounds. Cottenham has always attracted hunting and racing people from all quarters and among the early post-war riders were show-jumpers Harry Llewellyn and Alan Oliver, and trainer Jack O'Donoghue. Among the horses to run was Oxo, winner of the 1959 Grand National. By 1962, the course was so popular that three divisions of the Open Race were run. Hugh and Betty Gingell's last runner as owners was Regal Slipper in the mid-1960s, but their involvement with running the course – as well as farming the land, to say nothing of hunting the hounds – meant they remained fully involved.

In the latter years of her mastership, Betty Gingell shared the horn with her first whip, Miss Clare Williams, and, in spite of many bones broken over the years, barely ever missed a day. Her reputation hunting across the Cambridgeshire fens will live on for generations. Captain James Barclay says of her, 'There are not many people who could breed to such a high standard, all quality animals who not only won in the show-ring but also performed properly in the field; very few people breed both horses and hounds, and she was highly regarded. Her husband was almost a Denis Thatcher, an incredibly good man with the fen farmers; they were a truly sporting family.'

Part of Betty Gingell's love of hunting was finding, bringing on and showing heavyweight hunters during the summer – all as a prelude, of course, to hunting them. One, His Grand Excellency, retired from showing at twelve, but then carried Betty Gingell for the following seven consecutive Opening Meets and Boxing Days.

VII The North

There are times in one's life when one knows one is mad, even when doing what one loves. One such occasion for me was sitting on a horse on top of the Cheviots, with a searing gale biting through maximum thermal underwear, surrounded by bogs, rocks and ravines. Ice was on the dewponds and pockets of white frost made the heather seem in bloom. A buzzard circled overhead but there was little other visible wildlife. Macho men banged their hands together in a vain effort to keep warm, in spite of the pre-hunting warmer of whisky mixed with cherry brandy, known as Percy's Special.

Martin Letts, College Valley

There used to be plenty of foxes in that day's stretch of country but, in the mid-1990s, it was being turned into a grouse shoot and four gamekeepers were employed, resulting in very few. However, no one had told the hounds that as, climbing ever higher, they bounced through the heather, noses down, sterns waving, fanning their way forward ever eager. Up front with them, his big frame astride a faithful hunter, was Master and huntsman Martin Letts, quietly encouraging them. 'Martin is one of the five best huntsman in England,' a follower said proudly, 'another is Ronnie Wallace, and it doesn't matter about the other three.'

The mounted field picked their way carefully behind hounds and huntsman. The bright sunshine belied the bitterness of the cold so that even the magnificent views were difficult to appreciate. Heads remained bent, hooves avoided boulders and peat trenches alike. It was easy to imagine an invading army stealing across the landscape, with here and there the heather and crags giving way to a sea of white grass, dissected by bubbling burns spilling downwards. Old hill forts abound and only the conifer plantations are new.

Martin Letts, a man of few superfluous words, issued an instruction. He is foxwise, and told us to string out in line abreast, as if beating. Moments later a fox jumped up in front of us. It is a sight that never palls, and sets hearts a-drumming. Suddenly the circulation began to flow again, hands came

painfully back to life, and adrenalin took over. Fear of the uncertain terrain vanished as we set off in pursuit of hounds, over the moors, down a ravine and up the other side. For a moment it looked as if the fox was heading back for the top of the Cheviots but, mercifully for the faint-hearted, he swung down over the burn, through a remote farmstead and out on to a stony track. A considerable check followed until hounds hit off the line heading down the road towards lower land.

Martin Letts turned to his field again. 'This is going to be a slow hunt now and it's likely to be our only fox of the day. He now has at least a fifteen-minutes start on us. Please allow the hounds to settle to the line,' he called to a field keen to be in on the action. If they were too eager and crowded the hounds before they were truly on to the line, any hope of a good hunt would be ruined.

One of the field spotted the fox high up on a scree. Charlie stopped and nonchalantly looked around him as the lead hounds painstakingly followed the scent across the mountainous side. He knew he had plenty of time, and loped off down the other side towards pastures on the lower land.

Throughout, it was a pleasure to watch Martin's consummate skill with his hounds. Dedicated in the field and kennels, he is not averse to socializing at other times, over congenial tea after hunting, or with a stirrup cup at a host's house beforehand, or at any of the hunt's social functions. He has been Master and huntsman of the College Valley since 1964, a tenure of almost forty years, and his wife Eildon has been one of the joint-Masters since 1987.

It was her uncle, Sir Alfred 'Bill' Goodson, who founded the hunt in 1924 and who, on his retirement in 1964, handed over the pack to his successor, Martin.

Sir Alfred was one of the great hound breeders and also had a reputation for making sure the hunting was fun for the followers, too; on occasion he was known to play a tune such as 'Do ye ken John Peel' on his horn as he passed the field.

He fell in love with the North as a farm student on the Scottish side of the border; he had grown up hunting in Cheshire and Devon. To help him found his embryo pack, the Border gave him their land on the Cheviots, the North Northumberland gave him their hill country, and the Duke of Buccleuch's did likewise with their tract of hill land on the Scottish side. His foundation bitch, Goathland Rosebud, has many descendants today. Other hounds came from the Fells, for their suitability for hill hunting; the Cotley, the white West Country harriers; and the South and West Wilts, where Ikey Bell (see p. 100), as always, was generous in helping a young man get started and in giving advice on breeding a pack to suit the country – in this case, hard-driving and speedy with a good cry.

In 1982, the College Valley amalgamated with the North Northumberland, with Martin continuing to carry the horn. Here is a timeless piece of countryside, steeped in history and tradition, and the hunting often produces long runs with very few hindrances such as roads or towns. There are even moments when it seems as though life is in a time warp; for instance, it is the custom, before hunting, for women to be segregated in a different room from the men for the liquid brew.

In March 2003, Martin Letts retired from hunting the hounds after an excellent second half of the season. In Ian McKie he understandably believes he has found an ideal successor, for Ian has hunted the Bicester with Whaddon Chase hounds with élan since 1987. But on the future of hunting itself, Martin Letts is gloomier.

'I'm terribly alarmed,' he said, 'we went to sleep in the 1980s and became complacent with Maggie Thatcher in power, but that has boomeranged. It is not so bad for those of my age – and if there is a compromise, hunting will continue in countries like mine and the Fells – but it is hopeless for all the younger staff. As for the fabric of the countryside, it will collapse and the Government will be left with a problem similar to the one it already has in the inner cities.

'Luckily for my own hounds, they are well enough bred to ensure a demand for them abroad; I believe most of them will be able to go to America, where I do some hound judging.'

RUNNING ON

The dusk is down on the river meadows,
The moon is climbing above the fir,
The lane is crowded with creeping shadows,
The gorse is only a distant blur;
The last of the light is almost gone,
But hark! They're running!
They're running on!

The count of the years is steadily growing;
The Old give way to the eager Young;
Far on the hill is the horn still blowing,
Far on the steep are the hounds still strung.
Good men follow the good men gone;
And hark! They're running!
They're running on!

Will Ogilvie

THE FELLS

There are some glorious autumn mornings in the Cumbrian
Fells. The golds and ambers and russets mix with strands of pine
green on the steep hills, mirroring exact images into the smooth,
still waters of the lake below, making the moment twice as
magical. Further along, where a stream carves its way through a
valley, a pack of hounds is being unloaded from a small trailer.

Fox-hunting in the Fells is carried out on foot due to the steep
and boulder-strewn nature of the terrain. This hunting is not for
the unfit or faint-hearted, but the rewards come in the magnificent views, in the satisfaction at lambing time of killing known
predators and in the social scene.

The Fell packs of Coniston, Blencathra, Ullswater, Eskdale
and Ennerdale, Melbreak and Lunesdale have their own association, of which the North Lonsdale, Wensleydale and North

Eskdale and Ennerdale, Lake District

Pennine are associate members. The Eskdale and Ennerdale includes England's highest peak, Scafell, and the Isle of Man can be viewed from the west coast. The spot where its huntsman, Will Porter, died while hunting these hounds by Wastwater in 1952 is commemorated by a memorial stone; today, they are hunted by his grandson Edmund who, at eighteen, was the youngest huntsman when he took office in 1979, and is currently chairman of the Central Committee of Fell Packs.

Hunting in the Fells, where the foxes are big and strong, is part of a close-knit community life. When Michael 'Ossie' Osman was a lad from a non-hunting family growing up in Ambleside, a school pal took him out for a day with the Coniston under Anthony Chapman, considered by many to be one of the all-time best hill huntsmen.

He was an inspiration to youngsters, and Michael Osman considers meeting him when a child in the 1950s as a life-defining moment. Half a century later he still remembered him as a god who looked after the kids, and added, 'Anthony Chapman was like a dad to me.'

From the day that he met Anthony Chapman, Michael spent all his spare time in the kennels, learning, learning.

'Fell hunting is totally different to any other. Everyone is on foot, so hounds have to be independent, as well as bomb-proof in sheep,' Michael said. The hunting meets are set up differently, too, for instead of being scattered around the whole of a hunt country, they will have a complete week of hunting in one locality, and then move on to another. This stems from the days when there was little travel by car; people either walked, cycled or rode. For instance, the hunt staff and hounds would walk to, say, Langdale, on a Sunday, be met by a group of children and stay on farms. There would be a local area valley committee who organized not only the blanket hunting of the area during the week, but also all the functions, fund-raising and the village dance during the week, when a pig was likely to be roasted. This was fine for the local people whose big week of the winter it was, but for the huntsman it could be quite a

Hounds on a rugged cliff face in Eskdale and Ennerdale

stamina test as he went straight on to the next organized week with similar feasting and drinking to enjoy, as well as the hunting.

Although followers need to be fit, they learn to go steadily, to cut corners and to use hilltops as vantage points for viewing. The old hands will know the country backwards and occasional followers do best to follow them. Once a fell has been climbed, it is comparatively easy to walk along the ridge. When the air is bright and crisp, it is a particularly breath-taking experience. Way down below, even in winter, cars will be queueing at the bottleneck of Ambleside on their way to Kendal and Windermere, oblivious to those enjoying true nature several hundred feet above them.

The A66 cuts through the spectacular Blencathra country, but once deep into the Fells there are only small roads. There will be about fifty followers on a Saturday, a handful mid-week, and up to 200 over Easter. It is only since the Second World War that there have been a lot of foxes in the Fells, probably because so many of the big estates have become hotels and foxes have been left to flourish around them.

Sometimes a travelling dog fox will have come from as far as three villages away and may have 'hammered' a lambing farm, so a long, hard hunt may ensue. When the fox goes to ground, it is usually in a big rock borren, an accumulation of boulders that have rolled down the hillside, creating strongholds (much as big bale straw stacks have in arable countries). Because of the lambing, some hunting goes on until May, when hounds will go out at 5 a.m. to fields with new lambs who are in danger of attack from foxes. The huntsman will walk them round the perimeter of the field until the fox scent is picked up and the line followed.

At the end of the season, each hound returns to the handler who 'walked' it as a puppy, while the huntsman engages in a summer job, usually on a farm. There are very few paid whippers-in today, but those that help as amateurs are equally dedicated. The summer sees a continuation of the social scene, especially with the hound shows.

Anthony Chapman

A fox gone to ground in a borren

As well as Anthony Chapman, many Cumbrian people rate Johnny Richardson of the Blencathra as one of the great Fell huntsmen. He was an excellent hound breeder with an immense knowledge and memory. Today, the Blencathra is hunted by Barry Todhunter, who has done much to help in the battle to preserve hunting.

Probably the best-known Fell hunter of all time was John Peel, immortalized in song, and the first recorded huntsman of the Blencathra, although almost certainly hunting in the area is as old as the hills. John Peel, born in 1776 and one of thirteen children, was a Cumbrian through and through. He was a man of Caldbeck, a bigger Fell village than some, north of the lakes and south of Carlisle, with a stream trickling through it and a village pond. He spent all his life there and lived for hunting and the country life, as well as for his wife, Mary, with whom he eloped in traditional style: he rode over to her village in the dead of night, assisted her as she climbed out of her window, and together they rode to Gretna Green. The couple was

The huntsman of the Blencathra Foxhounds, Johnny Richardson (centre)

married for fifty-five years and had thirteen children.

Throughout that time, John Peel hunted the Blencathra hounds – many of those in today's pack are direct descendants – and earned his living by horse dealing. When hunting in the cultivated low farms, he would ride a 14.3hh pony; if the fox ran to the hills, he would dismount and continue on foot. Tall and robust, he thought nothing of walking 40 miles in a day, much of it steep. He was protected from the weather by a thick, grey coat woven from the local Herdswick sheep. It was in 1832 that he

and a friend, John Graves, were enjoying one of their convivial post-hunting evenings when Graves, listening to a lullaby being sung to his son, rewrote the words of it as 'D'you ken John Peel with his coat so grey?' and so immortalized his friend.

At the age of seventy-eight, John Peel came home from a day's hunting near Bassenthwaite feeling unwell, and he died a week later. Some 3,000 mourners attended his funeral at Caldbeck church and as the coffin passed by the kennels, the hounds chorused their farewell in musical unison.

Barry Todhunter leading the Blencathra Hunt

D'ye ken John Peel with his coat so grey?
D'ye ken John Peel at the break of day?
D'ye ken John Peel when he's far, far away –
With his hounds and his horn in the morning?

Yes, I ken John Peel and Ruby, too,
Ranter and Royal and Bellman as true,
From the drag to the chase, from the chase to the view,
From the view to the death in the morning.

'Twas the sound of his horn called me from my bed,
And the cry of his hounds has me oft-times led
For Peel's view holloa would awaken the dead
Or a fox from his lair in the morning.

And I've followed John Peel both often and far,
O'er the rasper-fence and the gate and the bar,
From Low Denton-Holme up to Scratchmere Scar,
Where we vied for the brush in the morning.

D'ye ken that bitch whose tongue was death?
D'ye ken her sons of peerless faith?
D'ye ken that a fox, with his last breath,
Curs'd them all as he died in the morning.

Then here's to John Peel with my heart and soul,
Come fill – fill to him another strong bowl,
And we'll follow John Peel through fair and through foul,
While we're waked by his horn in the morning.

too many, crowded on to the ferry. One horse, joint-Master Sir Charles Slingsby's Saltfish, became restless and kicked out, making the other horses veer to one side, causing the ferry to 'turn turtle'. Sir Charles almost reached the bank but was overpowered by the water; another man reached the steep bank but fell back into the water. Another seized the ferry chain and did manage to haul himself, hand over hand, to safety. On the bank side, heroic rescue efforts were being made. William Ingliby of Ripley Castle, venue of the hunt ball, tore off his coat and plunged in, but the waters were in full flow and he only narrowly avoided being drowned in the strong current. Mr Clare Vyner and Captain Preston made similar attempts to no avail. Only minutes after they had boarded the ferry, Sir Charles and five others, including the kennel huntsman and both ferrymen, had drowned, along with twelve horses. The accident naturally cast a gloom over the entire district, and is spoken of still; Saltfish's tail remains in the home of local dairy farmer Len Steele.

MAKING IT LOOK EASY

Tommy Normington is another through and through professional born into hunting. There have been many times when, watched from a distance by the mounted field, he would trot his horse up to a set of rails in a hedge and pop over. It would look so easy that the waiting riders would assume it could be only a small fence, but when they arrived, they'd find a substantial, solid obstacle. Such was the huntsman's natural horsemanship and the confidence he bestowed upon his horse.

Tommy is an elfin man, all smiles, full of fun, with slightly prominent ears and a small, slim figure. Only the fingers give him away, so swollen and gnarled with arthritis that eventually, after several operations, he was forced into retirement in 1995.

When he was a young man starting in hunt service, his mentor, Jack Simister, huntsman of the Fitzwilliam, taught him to 'see a fly from a mile away, let alone a fox!' Jack Simester, also responsible for setting Jim and Clary Webster, Tim Langley and Bryan Pheasey on the hunting ladder, made National Service pale in terms of discipline.

YORK AND AINSTY

Early in 1869, a 'large and brilliant field' of the York and Ainsty Hunt gathered in front of Stainley House, some sixty years before the hunt split permanently into two, North and South. Gentlemen in highly polished boots, svelte top hats and swish tailcoats riding beautifully turned-out horses partook of the port and admired the ladies riding side-saddle. It was 'February Filldyke' time and there had been a lot of rain, but there was no hint that this would be anything other than an ordinary hunting day. The first covert drew blank, but hounds screamed away from the second and were enjoying a 'capital run' when the fox crossed the swollen, 50-yard-wide River Ure.

In the heat of the chase – and many know the feeling – the leaders, the huntsman, the Master, the thrusters, hailed the ferrymen from Newby Hall to transport them across. Too many, far

OVERLEAF: *Lunesdale huntsman John Nicholson in the Lake District, north-west England*

'But,' recalls Tom, 'he was the greatest influence on my life.'

When Tom was born in 1937, his father, Jim, was second whipper-in to the Grove in Nottinghamshire. The family moved to the York and Ainsty North, where the young Tom, whose previous riding experience was sitting on the workhorse returning from a day's combine harvesting during the Second World War, was put up on ponies of all description by a local dealer. A natural lightweight with good hands, Tom was a horseman from then on – though he might have been a footballer: 'Yes, I had a chance with Charlton,' he says. But, incredible though it may seem now in the twenty-first century, he discovered he could earn more as a huntsman – 'and that was always my first love.'

While at York, he remembers setting off with the other hunt horses at 3 a.m., trotting down Blossom Street in York, past the station, under the city wall, over the River Ouse and by the beautiful Minster itself, hacking on out the other side to reach the meet.

A few days before his fifteenth birthday, Tom began work in the Blankney Hunt stables in Lincolnshire, and then moved on to the Fitzwilliam. There, he escorted retired huntsman Tom Agutter in the hunting field, 'another man who taught me so much'.

National Service not only 'made a man' of the impish Tom, but it also saw him riding regularly in the famous Kings' Troop Ride, holding the coveted lead driver position. Like many hunting riders, Tom wasn't keen on dressage riding (which doesn't make his talent any the less), but one German horse

Tommy Normington, all smiles and a thorough professional, 1989

Border foxhounds in Northumberland

would suddenly go into immaculate dressage movements. 'Trouble was, I not only didn't know what aid I'd given it to produce it, but I didn't know how to stop it either, which could be a bit awkward in the middle of the scissors manoeuvre!'

Tom returned to the Fitzwilliam after National Service as first whipper-in to Jack Simister. Once a fortnight he would have Sunday 'off' – that is to say, from 2 p.m., having first shown the hounds to any of the Fitzwilliam houseguests. He remembers, 'Jack Simister showed me what hunt service was about and how it should be done, how to be ambidextrous with the whip, turning and guiding, not hitting, hounds with either hand.'

Tom first came to the Grafton in Northamptonshire with his delightful bride, Ann, as first whipper-in to Joe Miller, 'the kindest, nicest man to work for you could imagine, and I carried on learning under him.' A post as kennel-huntman and first whipper-in took Tom up his next rung at the Tynedale, an all-grass country hunted with superb direction by one of the finest amateurs, George Fairbairn. Tom remembers him as 'the finest huntsman I have ever seen hunt a pack of hounds.' Joe passed away in September 2002.

In 1972, after as good a grounding as one can get, coupled with an innate love of hounds and hunting, it was back to the Grafton for Tom, initially under the command of its renowned Master Colonel Neil Foster, and then to take over the horn from the retiring huntsman, Joe Miller. 'Colonel Foster was much respected, and a good Master makes for good hunt servants, who in turn make good hunting,' Tom recalls.

Watching Tom with his hounds was always a pleasure in itself. 'But,' he says modestly, 'many casts termed brilliant are simply deductions, that's why amateurs often make good huntsmen, because they have the brains. Hounds have different characters, and a certain hound will tell you a certain thing.' And the most important thing about a day's hunting? 'That the people enjoy it.'

SCOTLAND

Hunting in Scotland is even more of a minority sport than elsewhere in the British Isles. Most of its ten hunts are close to the English border, and fishing, stalking and shooting probably have a bigger following. Yet hunting was, of course, a time-honoured part of Scottish country life until a rookie Parliament, new, naïve and with no second chamber, took it upon itself to ban it, ahead of almost any other, dare one say it, more important legislation.

There were the by now familiar protest marches: Edinburgh on 16 December 2001, for instance, in which some 15,000 staunch defenders of the sport wound their way from The Meadows and over the Royal Mile to King's Stable Road. But somehow one felt it was futile and, in August 2002, the act became law. The best chance, it seems, is to have the Protection of Wild Mammals (Scotland) Act overthrown in Europe.

As the new law stands, hounds may be used to flush a fox from a covert; it must then be shot by waiting marksmen. Only if it escapes wounded may the hounds be sent after it. This way, many more foxes are killed and those that have shotgun wounds but are not caught by the hounds are most likely to die slowly and painfully. And they say traditional fox-hunting, where the fox is either killed instantly or escapes unharmed, is cruel!

Many of the ten Scottish packs have become 'gun packs', but, sadly, the historic Dumfriesshire Hunt hounds have disbanded. The unique black and tan hounds were the result of breeding with French hounds in the 1920s and were famous for their loud cry, which could be heard in dense woodland. Some of the pack have gone back to France as well as to England and Ireland, but their loss to Scotland in general and to the Dumfriesshire in particular is little short of tragic.

The hunt's principal landowner and former Master for many years, Major Sir Rupert Buchanan-Jardine, felt compelled, reluctantly, not to allow the hounds over his 20,000-acre estate near Lockerbie, as he could be prosecuted for doing so if they were part of an illegal mounted hunt. It was a decision he took with great personal sadness and regret as he acknowledged the sport was an integral part of country life. He emphasized the decision was forced on him by the Scottish Parliament, something the disheartened hunt understood and accepted.

At the Berwickshire, the Master and huntsman, Jeremy Whaley, tried to compromise. He took out the foxhounds strictly according to the new law once a week, then, in an endeavour to raise money for them, he acquired some bloodhounds that he took out twice a week, enabling mounted followers to have a bit of a spin and some fun on their horses. In April 2003, the hunt split into two, the foxhounds becoming a separate entity from the bloodhounds, now named the Border Bloodhounds.

As a child, Jeremy Whaley was an ardent 'anti'. Brought up in Buckinghamshire, he loved animals and desperately wanted a pony. Eventually, he 'nicked' one off his older brother's girlfriend and had great fun playing cowboys and Indians with his mates. These friends used to go hunting with the Vale of Aylesbury and eventually, when he was about twelve or thirteen years old, Jeremy was persuaded to go with them. He recalls his first day. 'I sat all day on the edge of the saddle, waiting to witness the fox being "ripped to pieces" and to see "cruel, barbaric, sadistic" people, based on all the propaganda I'd been spoon-fed. Instead, I found everyone charming and kind.' Before long, Jeremy was completely hooked. In particular, it was the evident bond between the huntsman, Jim Bennett, and the hounds that caught him.

From school in Hampshire, Jeremy Whaley hunted with the Hursley, and then went on to the New Forest to manage a riding school. There, perhaps inevitably, he also became an amateur whip to the New Forest Hunt, where he was fortunate in serving under the great hound breeder and huntsman, Sir Newton Rycroft, largely influential, along with Ikey Bell, for infusing the Welsh long-haired blood into the modern foxhound. In the mid-1980s Jeremy became a joint-Master and the huntsman for three seasons, followed by a six-year spell with the Chiddingfold, Leconfield and Cowdray.

From there, it was up to Scotland in 1994 with his wife Lucy to take on the Berwickshire, believed to be Scotland's oldest pack, probably founded in the early 1600s.

He says, 'Hunting is my life, but I am not prepared to compromise my principles or to break the law. I believe this Act will be turned round in the courts eventually, the Government case is so weak, and if there is any justice in this world, then we will win.'

'I hope so,' he adds with feeling.

THE BOLD BUCCLEUCH

The bold Buccleuch are a Northern crew –
What you call a provincial pack –
And they do indeed hunt near the Tweed,
But nothing of style they lack,
Nothing of pace or love of the chase,
And the best man has plenty to do
If he wishes to ride from Salenside
In the lead of the bold Buccleuch.

If you're anxious for sport of the genuine sort
In a country of stone wall and thorn,
You'll have plough, grass, and heath with the Earl of Dalkeith
And the right man to carry the horn.
You'll return to the Shires and the rattle of wires
With the wish that you'd nothing to do
But for ever to ride with the hills at your side
In the wake of the bold Buccleuch.

Will Ogilvie

The whole Border area is utterly beautiful, as I found on a visit to the Duke of Buccleuch's, a famous ducal pack, in the 1990s. The setting for the meet was itself historic; it was held at Bemersyde House, home of Earl and Countess Haig, which had been given to the Earl's father by a grateful nation after the First World War, when, as Commander-in-Chief of the British forces in France, he had broken the Hindenberg Line. In 1921, he helped found the Royal British Legion to improve the welfare of ex-servicemen, for whom the Earl Haig Fund raises money every November by selling poppies for Remembrance Sunday.

Much of the hunting that day was by the banks of the majestic River Tweed and around Wallace's Monument, a huge monument built in honour of Sir William Wallace, a Scottish patriot who led a revolt against English rule in 1297. He assumed the title Governor of Scotland, but he was defeated a year later by Edward I and executed.

Later, hounds ran below Scott's View, a local beauty spot named in honour of the Tweed's illustrious poet and early novelist, Sir Walter Scott.

Whether or not hounds killed that day, or even if there was much of a hunt, I don't recall, but I do remember coming away enriched. These are the sort of experiences that will be lost to ordinary lay followers of a hunt, be they on foot, car or horseback, should hunting be banned.

VIII Central Southern England

Wiltshire, Gloucestershire and Oxfordshire are parts of southern England that conjure up pretty English villages, grand estates, green fields, the lofty beauty and mellow stone of the Cotswolds, the M4 corridor, wealth, and hunting that is as good as in the Shires.

The Beaufort Hunt at Badminton, *Edmund Havell*

THE FARQHAR–FANSHAWE CONNECTION

There are several four-days-a-week packs, such as the Beaufort, the VWH, the Warwickshire, the Heythrop and the Bicester with Whaddon Chase. And the less fashionable hunts can be just as much fun. Hunting here is full of friendliness, camaraderie, good sport and tradition, often going back generations.

Nobody better illustrates this than Ruth, Lady Dulverton, who was born a Farquhar and married a Fanshawe. Few hunting pedigrees can be more impeccable than that. Today the nonagenarian lives in the idyllic Vale of Pewsey village of Milton Lilbourne in the Tedworth country, itself steeped with family connections.

Lady Dulverton's brother was Sir Peter Farquhar, born in 1905, who earned a reputation as the greatest breeder of the modern foxhound. He, perhaps more than any other, owed much to the advice and wisdom of the renowned foxhunter Ikey Bell.

Born in the 1880s, Isaac Bell was an American, brought up in Paris, with a lifelong passion for English fox-hunting. As a boy, he would be seen galloping round the Champs-Elysées on a carriage horse, blowing a hunting horn and 'hunting' an imaginary pack of hounds. He devoured all the reading he could find on hunting and, most unusually for a child, especially one from a non-hunting background, he was fascinated by hound pedigrees.

Sir Peter Farquhar

Educated in England, at Harrow, he could sample the hunting first-hand, but he soon found that many of the hounds were large, cumbersome and slow. They had not moved on with the faster hunting that had come in with the Inclosure Acts, and many were bred for the show-ring rather than utility.

In 1903, he moved to Ireland and, still in his twenties, hunted the Galway Blazers and then the Kilkenny, where he began to use the longer-coated Welsh hound blood with excellent results. Purists considered this heresy but, a century on, his work has been more than vindicated. Luckily, a move back to England, to the South and West Wilts, and his friendship with Sir Peter Farquhar at the nearby Portman kennels, meant the new style of breeding was brought to England, too.

As a huntsman, he was full of wisdom. He acknowledged that hounds know more about hunting than a huntsman; he was a great believer in having hounds fully fit and in great condition, starting their exercise much earlier in the summer than many kennels; he realized the importance of gaining the trust of a young hound and of making it up to him if he made a mistake. And, thankfully, he did not like shouting at hounds as if they were deaf, knowing their hearing to be acutely sharp.

Sir Peter moved to the Tedworth on the Wiltshire–Hampshire border in 1927 and met Ikey Bell two years later. Both men agreed that the foxhound of the day was far too cumbersome, large and slow to be a proficient fox-catcher. So they started breeding lighter, more active hounds, and their legacy lives on today.

While at the Tedworth, Sir Peter enjoyed the services of two amateur whippers-in, his brother Reggie and another serving soldier friend, Dick Fanshawe. Thus it was that his only sister, Ruth, met and subsequently married Dick Fanshawe, who was later to become Master of the South Oxfordshire and of the North Cotswold. She subsequently married Tony, Lord Dulverton, Master of the North Cotswold and, later, the Heythrop; she was married to both gentlemen for thirty years, and was herself a joint-Master of the North Cotswold.

By the outbreak of the Second World War, Dick Fanshawe was hunting the South Oxfordshire hounds (amalgamated in 1970 with the Hertfordshire and the Old Berkeley to form the Vale of Aylesbury). He went off to serve with distinction, leaving Ruth with son David at prep school, younger son Brian at home and a pack of hounds to keep going single-handedly as best she could. 'My grandchildren say to me now how wonderful it must have been for me to hunt a pack of hounds, but it was hard work,' she admits.

Feeding the hounds was one problem, solved, to some extent, by collecting sweepings from the local Huntley & Palmers biscuit factory near Oxford. 'But I would have to shake the troughs before feeding to listen for metal, and take out the various nuts and bolts that had been swept up, too. Some of them must have been eaten, but the hounds didn't seem to suffer any ill effects.'

Another difficulty was caused by the wartime blackout. 'We used to meet at ten in the morning to try to finish before dark, but that didn't always happen. There was one occasion when we were crossing a narrow, bridged causeway surrounded by water meadows, when a convoy approached. I called, "trot on", and thankfully all the hounds came.'

The field consisted of the occasional soldier home on leave, a number of women, the very old and the very young. 'Hounds mostly hunted themselves,' Lady Dulverton says modestly, but the redoubtable lady is made of strong British stuff that brooks no nonsense and does things properly.

Her younger son, Brian, had a highly distinguished hunting career as Master and huntsman, including of Ireland's Galway Blazers, the North Cotswold and the Cottesmore, serving the Shire pack for a memorable ten years from 1981 to 1991. He had a fine reputation for crossing the country and staying with hounds. His horses and hounds would do anything for him, though members of the human field may remember his own ability to 'give tongue'. He used to take out his entire pack of hounds on each hunting day, a very unusual practice, but it resulted in a superbly fit pack that was smaller in number than most. Tim Holland, who used to hunt with the North Cotswold before taking on the Emlyn beagles in Wales, remembers,

Captain Brian Fanshawe

'The result was a superb pack of athletes who were supremely confident in their ability to catch foxes. This was one of the mainstays of the consistently brilliant sport Brian Fanshawe showed.' Although most packs would retain plenty of 'spares', sitting on the bench with daily exercise is no substitute for hunting in the field.

Today, with the health and future of hunting ever at heart, Brian Fanshawe is secretary for the Council of Hunting Organisations, having before that run the Campaign for Hunting. Brian's cousin, Ruth Dulverton's nephew, is Captain Ian Farquhar, one of the greatest modern all-round ambassadors for the sport of fox-hunting, as well as huntsman and hound breeder.

The youngest of three sons, Ian grew up in the Portman kennels in Dorset, where he would sit cross-legged on the floor absorbing talk about hounds, their breeding and management, not only from his famous hunting father, Sir Peter, but also from Ikey Bell.

Although there were horses and ponies around, it was the hounds that were constantly part of family conversation and today, six decades or so on, his sheer love of these creatures is still self-evident.

Horses were secondary, though never mere tools of the trade, and Ian became a competent point-to-point rider and an expert polo player as a serving officer with the Queen's Own Hussars. He considers it imperative that the horses are well serviced and schooled for hunting, and over the years some of them have been as well loved as certain hounds, 'but I do look at them in a slightly different light.'

Ian met and married Pammy-Jane Chafer in 1974, while still serving. Her father, Charles Chafer, was Master of the Derwent hounds in North Yorkshire for thirty years. The wedding was arranged for 5.30 p.m., as it was only natural that the two men, bridegroom and father of the bride, should get in a full day's hunting first. 'But of course the bride mustn't see the groom on her wedding day so she wasn't allowed to come – father-in-law agreed,' Ian recalls with a chuckle.

One of the guests at the wedding was old friend Alex Bond, at the time field-Master with the Bicester; unfortunately, he is now confined to a wheelchair following a point-to-point fall. He happened to mention that a vacancy for Master and huntsman was available with the Bicester, situated in the south Midlands. At this stage, Ian had never hunted any pack of hounds, let alone a prestigious four-days-a-week pack. But at the airport, as he set out for his honeymoon, Ian rang the chairman. An 'absolutely marvellous' twelve years followed.

The Bicester, covering much of Oxfordshire and parts of Buckinghamshire, south Northamptonshire and a little piece in Warwickshire, was still a surprisingly wild country with 75 per cent grass, very little wire, big, challenging country to cross and a plentiful supply of strong, healthy foxes – a hunter's paradise. Throughout, Ian was admirably assisted by professional kennel huntsman Bryan Pheasey, and at first they both hunted the hounds twice a week. 'Bryan was wonderful; he taught me absolutely everything I know. There was no better, nicer, braver, kinder man – and the same went for his wife, Nora.'

Before long, Ian was breeding the sort of hounds he most wanted. Sir Newton Rycroft, another renowned hound breeder, continued the kind of advice that Ian had been given by his father and Ikey Bell as a small child and, soon, he introduced some Welsh blood into the pack, just as his own father had done before the war. He already had New Forest Medig, with the longer, hairy coat of the Welsh hounds.

Some 'spies' suggested he visit the Vale of Clettwr Hunt high up in the Welsh Hills, where Trevor Jones was Master and huntsman and the pack had an excellent reputation for fox-catching. He took home a bitch called Fairy to see if she would hunt equally well in the more open Bicester country. Not only does his face still light up at the mention of her name, but he also has some of her descendants with him at the Beaufort. Her second litter, by Bicester Freeman (who was by Whaddon Grimstone) produced, in 1976, the great Farmer, an outstanding dog who bred many good hounds, some being crossed with Medig lines. Ian brought one of Farmer's sons, Farrier, with him

to the Beaufort. 'What intrigued me,' he says, 'was how tightly Farrier could turn with a fox, he had a very good nose.'

In a world that is full of characters, Ian has stored away many hilarious memories, wild days (and probably nights) and treasures the 'wonderful, friendly lot' that make up the hunting fraternity. Ian has an outgoing, friendly personality that makes any stranger feel welcome and his sheer love of life is infectious.

His best hunting, especially in terms of long hunts, came in the 1970s, with 1979, when he was still with the Bicester, standing out in particular. That season of good scenting produced twenty-six points of more than 5 miles with, in February alone, four hunts of more than 7 miles. There was a day when they were due to be hunting in woods and Pammy-Jane was having a first, short day following the birth of her daughter, Victoria. But a fox was away from a stick pile close to a pub and there followed a 7 1/2-mile point, across a tricky piece of country and then on out into the Bicester's best; eventually, hounds had to be stopped by a railway line. Second horses arrived, Pammy-Jane went home and, before they knew it, hounds were off again, this time on a 5 1/2-mile point right up to a cemetery on the edge of Oxford where, once again, hounds had to be stopped. On another day during this spell, hounds scored a 4 1/2-mile point on a slow scent; they hacked back to that day's area and promptly hunted a 5-mile point. The process was repeated, they hacked back and were off again, this time for a 6-mile point.

In the 1970s there were the biggest changes in the countryside. It was then that Ian saw the effect on the Midlands and south of the EEC wheat bonanzas. In the Bicester country alone the amount of grassland was reduced to 30 per cent with most of the rest sown to wheat and many miles of hedgerows pulled out. 'More damage was done to the structure of middle England than Hitler ever did,' Ian Farquhar declares. The dairy farm next door to him had been 160 acres divided into fourteen fields, but when it was sold, it became just two fields, all of it sown to wheat.

This sort of agricultural change may have been one of the reasons Ian was considering taking a pack in Northumberland; others were a love of the wild country up there and, of course,

Captain Ian Farquhar with the Bicester hounds, before his move to the Beaufort

the proximity of Pammy-Jane's family in North Yorkshire. But fate intervened.

In 1985, the 10th Duke of Beaufort, known universally as Master, died. Ian, whose father was a cousin to the duke and both families being great friends, was required to go and hunt the Beaufort hounds, one of the world's most elite packs. One imagines it was almost equal to a royal command. Ian, of course, was up to the challenge. Before long he was producing good sport and not only maintaining but also improving the famous pack of hounds, notable for their size.

It is easy enough to breed big, lumbering, slow hounds, but the skill has been to infuse and maintain speed as well. Here, there is a parallel to breeding big hunters: it is easy enough to get size but to inject quality in the form of speed and agility is much harder and consequently is greatly sought after.

Ian had brought Farrier with him from the Bicester and within about five years he felt he had the pack as he had been striving for. There were, of course, already incredibly strong bloodlines, some of them going back to 1743. The first volume of the Foxhound Kennel Stud Book did not appear until 1800, but it included several appendices tracing pedigrees from earlier years. Ian says, 'The foxhound is probably the most chronicled animal in the world, tracing back some fifty-four generations.' The 10th Duke's breeding for size and stamina continues to come out, but the last thirty years have also seen a bigger influx of outcross blood than anywhere else in England. The stallion hounds that have most influenced Ian's breeding have been Medig from the New Forest in the 1970s, Farrier in the 1980s and, currently, David Davies Bouncer, a pure Welsh hound.

Ian is an excellent tutor with young hounds, believing in the philosophy of notching up 'flying hours'. At the start of the new season every autumn, he will take them out three times a week for five to six hours at a time rather than twice a week for a couple of hours. That way they will have experienced sixteen hours instead of four. He adopts the same principle with horses, believing too many are underworked and over-fresh.

Ian loves living and hunting in the Beaufort. Spanning parts of Gloucestershire, Wiltshire and Somerset, it is a land of dairy farms, hedges and stone walls. Its kennels are at Badminton, home of the Duke of Beaufort, and host to the world's premier three-day event. 'Contrary to what one might have expected, there are no factions; they are lovely people, with a very friendly atmosphere, lots of laughs and parties. The farmers are brilliant and make up the backbone of the hunt. More farmers follow on horseback here than in any other hunt in England. The attitude of the farming fraternity towards hunting is, if anything, even stronger.' Refusing even to contemplate a future without the Beaufort hounds, Ian says, 'The sport of hunting is so defensible that I cannot believe that at the end of the day common sense will not prevail.'

The late 10th Duke of Beaufort, 1973

To the Farmers

When we bid a farewell to the season
And turn out our hunters to grass,
'Twould be surely the blackest of treason
To go without filling a glass
To the men who have furthered our pastime
By lending their fields for the fun!
Here's 'The Farmers' – Once, twice and a last time –
And 'Grandfather, father, and son!'

Looking back on the season that's ended,
We blush for our track in the seeds,
For the fences we left to be mended,
And the damage we did in the Swedes;
And so, when we know there's no brooding
And the mending is cheerfully done,
Let us drink to the farmers; including
The grandfather, father, and son!

From that rattling good day in November
Up to yesterday's wonderful burst
There is scarcely a run we remember
When a farmer was other than first.
It's because when the pace becomes clinking
They can ride with us second to none
That we drink – with our hearts in the drinking –
'The Farmers! Sire, grandsire, and son!'

Will Ogilvie

Backbone Men

It is the unsung heroes, hunting's 'backroom boys', who make up the backbone of the sport. Unfailingly, they live for it, in spite of the toil and distinctly unglamorous chores they perform, and meeting any one of them enriches one's life. Imagine a job that involves swilling down smelly, messed kennel floors day in, day out, changing hounds' beds, preparing feeds, nursing the lame, shooting or picking up fallen stock many miles distant and skinning them, and working outdoors in all weathers, yet includes lunching with Prince Charles or holding the Queen Mother's umbrella for her when she visited the kennels.

Colin Day has worked for more than forty years as kennel-man to the Bicester with Whaddon Chase and, despite his 'job description' lives a remarkably rich life that includes annual trips to California. Colin, the son of a small tenant farmer in the Croome country near the River Severn, has only ever had two jobs: four years as second kennelman with the Old Berks and the remainder with the Bicester. Hounds had been a major influence in his childhood, too, when he walked puppies and helped to whelp bitches for the Croome Hunt.

It is this helping to bring new life into the world that has given him the greatest satisfaction. He thinks nothing of sitting up all night to help whelping bitches, talking to them, soothing, nursing, keeping them company to let them know they are not alone and that someone cares. During his many years at the Bicester kennels at Stratton Audley, Oxfordshire, which houses some 120 hounds at any given time, the number that he has not see born personally can be counted on the fingers of one hand.

Colin always takes the same caring view of a far less pleasant task, that of dispatching someone's favourite hunter, something he is requested to do personally by those who know it will be the kindest thing. His biggest interest outside hunting is racing, and the view of the knacker wagon parked outside the betting shop became so familiar in Bicester that even the traffic warden allowed him a few moments each day in which to place his 20-pence units.

It was highly appropriate, therefore, that the hunt marked his thirtieth anniversary with tickets for the Cheltenham Gold Cup and Champion Hurdle for him and his wife, Marie, who had turned up as a 'teenage skinhead in bovver boots' looking for a job twenty-eight years before and never left. Ian Farquhar, whom Colin rates as a friend as well as former Master, arranged tickets for a 'lunch we'll never forget' hosted by Prince Charles at the Barbican in London for Colin and Marie, and Bryan and Nora Pheasey.

Bryan Pheasey was quoted as saying 'life begins after sixty' when, in the twilight of his long and distinguished career in hunt service, he suddenly found himself hunting the Bicester hounds four days a week. He had already been an indispensable right-hand-man to Ian Farquhar in what Bryan described as the best twelve years of his life. At the start of Ian's career, Bryan had hunted the bitch pack twice a week until Ian took over both bitches and mixed packs for the four days a week. When Ian moved on to the Beaufort, and then an 'interregnum' following the retirement of his successor, the Hon. Luke White, Bryan was asked to stand in. It was a great accolade for a man in his twenty-fifth and retirement season with the pack. One of nature's gentlemen, he had already earned the admiration and respect of all those within the hunt and many outside it during his quarter of a century at the Stratton Audley kennels.

Bryan grew up near Buxton, Derbyshire, where his father was a stud groom, and soon Bryan was following hounds on foot. The interest never left him, and when he was demobbed from the Air Force after the Second World War, he became whipper-in to the High Peak Harriers under enthusiastic huntsman George Steele for six seasons.

There followed a season with the Fitzwilliam under Jack Simister – a fine tutor of future huntsmen – and five with the Grafton under Joe Miller, another who had a renowned reputation for instilling hunting lore in young men. Bryan's chance as kennel huntsman and first whipper-in then came up at the Avon Vale, a hunt he remembers fondly for the friendliness of the people and the lovely countryside.

From there, with his and Nora's family having grown to two boys and two girls, Bryan jumped at the opportunity to hunt

Bicester huntsman, Bryan Pheasey

ABOVE: *Bryan Pheasey's last meet at Newton Morrell, 1989: John Kennelly, Tommy Normington, Peter Jones and Billy Marples*

RIGHT: *Martin Thornton leading his hounds from a meet at Belvoir Castle*

hounds two days a week with the Bicester and Warden Hill, before it amalgamated with the Whaddon Chase.

So began twenty-five memorable years, of which the twelve with Ian Farquhar hold outstanding memories. 'As well as great sport, everything worked well, we were even lucky with the weather, with great scenting in open season after open season,' he said, recalling those same magical long runs as Captain Farquhar. He also remembered the brilliant Fairy. 'She hunted like a dingbat and truly possessed "fox sense"; she never left a stone unturned to find a fox, then nothing would get her off the line.' When Bryan finally retired in the early 1990s, he and Nora settled

in a house in the same Oxfordshire village, Stratton Audley. It is a typical English village, where Ian Farquhar instituted an annual hunt carol service in the village church, something that was brought to Badminton for the first time in 2001.

Bryan was succeeded as professional huntsman by Martin Thornton, who came from the Zetland in Yorkshire and in 1992 went on to become the admired huntsman of the prestigious Belvoir hounds at the Duke of Rutland's magnificent kennels in Leicestershire.

Sidney Bailey was literally born and bred to hunting. He was born in the Braes of Derwent, an attractive country in

Sidney Bailey on his way to a meet, 1998

Northumberland, where his grandfather, Alfred Littleworth, was the renowned huntsman. His father, Tom Bailey, became kennelman to Captain Ronnie Wallace, so it was down south to the Heythrop country where the young Sidney did what little schoolwork he couldn't avoid.

However, at fourteen, he was chucked out of school for missing too much to go hunting, and at fifteen he was working as second whipper-in at the Heythrop kennels, before becoming first whip to Nimrod Champion at the Ledbury. Today, his name is synonymous with the VWH (Vale of White Horse) Hunt in Wiltshire and Gloucestershire, where he has hunted the four-day-a-week pack for nearly four decades.

Out hunting, his cap will be pushed down low, but from under its peak his eyes are penetrating; the mouth is set in

Sidney Bailey showing young doghounds to judges Ian Farquhar and Michael Farrin at the VWH Hunt Puppy Show, 1996

concentration but still curves smilingly upwards at the corners, increasing the dimple in his chin. His back is upright, his hands low on his horse's withers, and he has the demeanour of unassuming confidence, born from decades of riding horses and hunting hounds.

At twenty, Sidney Bailey's first employment was with the VWH and only one year later, following the death of the hunts-man, John White, he found himself probably the youngest huntsman in the country. Then the hunt's amalgamation with the Cricklade resulted in a spell at the Wylye Valley (just as the lion pens were being erected at Longleat), but in 1966 Sidney was back at the VWH where, with the invaluable support of his wife, Carol, he has been ever since – as fine an ambassador to the sport as can be found.

IX Wales and the Welsh Borders

David Davies Hunt country is a forgotten, timeless piece of Britain, where for generations life has continued in time-honoured tradition, with loyalties held high for hunting, rugby and farming.

Lord Davies leading the David Davies field in the hills

David Davies' hunt terriers, with Jackie Harris

A WELSH LEGEND

Set in Powys, in the middle of Wales in the mountains above the upper reaches of the River Severn, its views stretch over the Cambrian Mountains and, on a clear day, to the Brecon Beacons 50 miles to the south, and to Cadair Idris in the north.

Hounds are its main asset, along with the humans at the helm. Family involvement since David Davies (later Lord Davies) founded it as a private pack at the start of the twentieth century continues with the current Lord Davies, aided by the exceptional huntsman of thirty seasons, David Jones; an amateur whip of forty seasons, the pipe-smoking Neville Owen; and a loyal local following that could be equalled, but not bettered, anywhere.

The first Lord Davies, having started in 1905 with a few draft hounds, mainly from the Tivyside, then bought some all-Welsh, rough-coated hounds to cross with English foxhounds. These produced the light-coloured, broken-coated hounds that have become famous for their cry and ability to hunt on their own – two essentials high in the hills where it is often impossible for man to be with them, either on foot or mounted.

The first Lord Davies died in 1944, his elder son was killed in action only a few months later, and after the Second World War the hunt became a subscription pack. However, the hounds stayed the property of Lord Davies, kennelled at the Davies home at Llandiam, with a Davies remaining as Master.

The present Lord Davies, also chairman of the Arts Council of Wales, has been Master since 1963 and has on occasions hunted the hounds himself, but in David Jones he has one of the country's best and most passionate of huntsmen who does nothing but good both for the sport and its image.

Born in a Merthyr Tydfel valley council house from a non-hunting family, it was forays out rabbiting that got David Jones hooked on country life, terriers (he now judges in America and is an internationally known breeder) and hunting. He recalls clearly the first time he ever went hunting. It was with the Sennybridge, another of Wales's small, hilly, afforested packs, and he can remember the name of the hound, Truly, who hit off the line of a fox after it had gone into a patch of rushes. His unwavering ambition became to hunt hounds himself one day.

He met his future wife, Sue, at fifteen, and at sixteen took her for her first day's hunting. They married in 1967, the year he first carried the horn for the Taf Fechan, newly formed by local farmers in the Brecon Beacons and hunted entirely on foot.

After five seasons, David was 'headhunted' by Lord Davies and has become something of a Welsh legend, completely at home mixing with all walks of life – 'there is no class distinction in hunting' – and speaking up in hunting's cause whenever and wherever he can. Leader of the Welsh core marchers in 1997, he cherishes the march flag, framed in oak for him by the hunt and signed by all the Welsh marchers. He speaks from the heart in defence of hunting and its way of life, and has presented his views at a number of official inquiries and public meetings.

Up in the hills of the David Davies country in Powys, the ever-fit David Jones still spends much of his time hunting hounds on foot. The hunt is there, he says, to give a service to local farmers plagued by foxes killing their lambs and, because of the terrain, the hounds not only have to be able to hunt unaided, but must also be 100 per cent steady with sheep.

From the back of a horse, one often takes a grandstand view as hounds hunt round an opposite hill. They will disappear from view and reappear five or ten minutes later, the sound of their music echoing across the valley. When horses are used, they are surprisingly smart – thoroughbreds rather than cobs – but they are surefooted and have the extra power and stamina for coping with the terrain. On top of the hills it is like moorland, with bogs and sheep tracks and ancient turf. In places there are outcrops of wind turbines, more than 100 in a cluster, monumental structures towering above the natural rocky outcrops and so noisy that few foxes rest beneath them.

'We have to breed hounds who can hunt by themselves,' explains David, 'whereas in England they have to breed hounds that can be picked up quickly because of the roads. But when our hounds are running there is no stopping them … It is wonderful to see a brilliant pack of hounds sticking to their fox.'

RUINED CASTLES AND CELTIC CROSSES

If you drive west as far as the M4 goes and then on for another hour, past ruined castles and Celtic crosses, to the ferry port at Haverfordwest, where a large supermarket vies for attention with the Cromwell-destroyed castle, you find yourself in Pembrokeshire Hunt country. There are many pretty inlets and coves on the coast while the Preseli Hills rise gently in the east. The land between is a patchwork quilt of small dairy farms, although there are not as many of those as there were, and sheep, interspersed with gorse, thorn, moor and rivers.

The huntsman here since 1989, Gary Barber, is as Welsh as the hunt and held in high local regard. He breeds his hounds with Exmoor, South Pembrokeshire and David Davies blood, and they work hard for him. He is also particularly good on the horn, having twice won the professional section of the Horse and Hound horn-blowing competition. A former Master of the hunt described him simply as 'one of the best huntsmen in Britain'.

Born in a Welsh valley, Gary went straight from school to the Gelligear Farmers, a small, steep, rugged hunt of moorland and forestry in Gwent and Mid Glamorgan. Gary loves Welsh hounds and says he has no intention of ever serving anywhere outside the principality. He and his wife, Julie, a caretaker, have four sons, all of them keen; one, Marc, is also a point-to-point rider.

The Pembrokeshire Hunt followers ride an assortment of equines and are themselves as motley a mix of country-loving people as can be imagined. Many are farmers and it is plainly evident that hunting and farming go hand in hand here. One of the field-Masters, Billy Green, was a 'goer' right up until his death in 2002 in his mid-seventies. Not only did he lead the field over the toughest of country, but also, before embarking on a long day in the saddle, he first tended his beef cattle and home-bred horses. His wife, Thora, helped to make ready his hunter in spite of having two plastic hips. At a nearby farm and trekking centre, 'granny' Eira Owen, also in her seventies, is the matriarch, but the hunting is now mostly done by her two

Hunting in Pembrokeshire

grandsons, Charles and Lawson. In their twenties, both are mad keen, with Charles being an amateur whip. Lawson and his wife, Penny, breed horses and run the trekking centre in summer and help all they can in the hunting field in winter. Two of the three Masters are sisters, Ruth Rees and Margaret Johns, daughters of a farmer, Mrs Sheila Vaughan, and both are married to farmers. Wyn Morris makes up the trio.

'THE MORNING THAT CHANGED MY LIFE'

One of the smartest hunts outside Leicestershire, with an ocean of grass and good fences, is the Sir Watkin Williams-Wynn's, known as the Wynnstay. Stretching between north Wales, Cheshire and Shropshire, it is peopled with farmers and foxhunters true.

Bert Loud moved to the Wynnstay as first whip in 1980, the year he got married. Spells with the Axe Vale and then the Exmoor, working under Captain Ronnie Wallace, laid the grounding for his move. But he was a small boy living in Devon when his uncle, Harry Lenthil, who was kennel huntsman to Sir Newton Rycroft, first took him hunting. 'That morning changed my whole life,' he recalls, 'and although I was clueless to what was really going on, it was all so thrilling.'

It has remained thrilling. When Harry moved to the Axe Vale Harriers, close to Bert's home, Bert spent every waking moment hunting, following the hounds up hill and down on his bicycle, quite often skipping school to do so. 'I knew my vocation was to be a hunt servant,' he says.

The Wynnstay Hunt and the country around it is clearly a part of the world that Bert Loud loves, especially the old English hounds that he admires for their 'determination, toughness and persistence'. Their breeding includes bloodlines from the Brocklesby, Waterford, Muskerry and Limerick.

He had many good seasons under Master and huntsman Robin Gundry, whose daughter, Polly, is champion point-to-point rider. When William Wakeham was offered a similar

Bert Loud at the Wynnstay

position, it was on condition that he retained Bert Loud as kennel huntsman, something the ex-army officer was only too happy to do.

A large and eclectic field includes numerous farmers, smartly turned out ladies and a splattering of nobility. There is Barry Woolham, a farmer and former Master, who has barely missed a single day's hunting with this three-day-a-week pack in more than thirty years (he once was obliged to attend a funeral), while the managing director of Aintree Racecourse, Charles Barnett, follows, usually on ex-racehorses, as often as work permits. Sharing the mastership with William Wakeham is Lord Daresbury who, as Peter Greenall, was a champion amateur rider. Steven Lloyd makes up the trio of Masters. The Watkin Williams-Wynn family has kept a pack of hounds on this part of

the Welsh borders since the mid-eighteenth century, although records only began in 1841 with the 7th Baronet. It is known that in 1758 the 4th Sir Watkin Williams-Wynn kept harriers and foxhounds, and it is believed that the 3rd Baronet was killed out hunting just a few years before that. The family connection has been maintained ever since.

BIRTH OF A HUNT

Although a comparatively young hunt, the Golden Valley had for its first half-century only one Master and huntsman, Mr Vivian Bishop. There had been hunting in the area since 1777, but in 1945 Vivian Bishop requested a loan of country from the Radnor and West Herefordshire Hunt to form the Golden Valley Hunt.

When some high profile amateur huntsmen and Masters were known for being somewhat wrathfully vocal in the field (albeit they are trying to help hounds hunt well and don't like having their fox headed and so on), Vivian Bishop maintained a reputation, in the words of hunt chairman Peter Cooper, for 'insistence on the virtues of courtesy and good manners, both in behaviour and language, that have made the Golden Valley the happy, friendly hunt is has always been'.

Vivian Bishop was born and bred in the area in 1911 and lived for hunting, farming (mostly livestock) and point-to-pointing. He and his wife, Hazel, and one of their daughters, Diana, were also first class point-to-point riders. In later years, he would hunt hounds off full brothers Humorous and Velvet Coat, then Diana would steer them to racing victory, sporting the Bishop colours of mauve and black. But hunting was always his first love.

He was whipping in to Captain Hope's Hounds that were then hunting in the area and carried the horn when he was twenty-five. Captain Hope's wife was killed out hunting in 1938 and the pack was not restarted after the Second World War. So it was that Vivian Bishop, who had served as a major in the Home Guard, sought permission to set up the Golden Valley after the war. He acquired eight couple of hounds and began hunting south of the River Wye. The object of the hunt was 'to provide sport and to destroy foxes in the district'.

He knew the country inside out, was always punctual at the meet and moved off on time. His way of hunting hounds was never to hurry through a draw, and to let them work out a check, casting around for themselves rather than the huntsman 'lifting' them. There was no shouting and no unnecessary hollering throughout the half-century he was in charge.

Vivian Bishop, Master of the Golden Valley Foxhounds since 1945

During its formative years, the hunt raised money through subscriptions and by running hunter trials, a hunt ball and a point-to-point, as well as founding a branch of the Pony Club, of which Hazel Bishop was district commissioner for its first forty-eight years. A limited number of tickets for the first hunt ball in 1946 cost 15s 6d (77 $^1/_2$p), including buffet supper. Dancing continued to 1 a.m. and a profit of £163 was made. By 1952, when the ball was attended by a record 240, dancing continued to the band music and hunting horns until 2.30 a.m.

PUPPY SHOWS

By that time, most of the social offshoots of hunting were well established. The annual Boxing Day meet was held in the local town centre, Hay-on-Wye. The puppy show is the traditional summer highlight of the hunt's calendar, an excuse to 'put on the finery' – ladies in hats and dresses, men in panamas and suits or blazers – when old friends meet out of season, and where that year's 'young entry', puppies of just over a year old, come under the scrutiny of two invited judges (most hunts will have one Master and one huntsman) and are shown 'on the flags', often a makeshift square in the middle of the roped-off kennel yard.

For weeks beforehand, the kennel staff will have been repainting the kennels and stables, tending the gardens and fencing, and generally giving the kennels their annual spruce up. It is above all an occasion to thank the local farmers for allowing the hunt over their land, and to thank the puppy walkers who will have looked after one or two puppies during their formative months, regardless of dug-up flower beds, chewed furniture and the best sofa taken over for daytime snoozes.

PAGAN

When out with the Duhallow, wherever I stand
There's always one muzzle that searches my hand,
And coming up stealthily gently will spread
My fingers and palm till they rest on his head,

Looks up at me smiling, 'I'll never forget
Those days as a puppy, I spent as your pet,
The children adored me, we raced round the lawn,
I swam in the river and rolled in the corn.

I tore out the fleece of your best bedroom rug,
And many a hole in flower beds I dug.
The bantams went flying (I murdered a pair),
And left my tooth marks in a dining room chair.

And now my fifth season draws on to its close,
I've grey round my muzzle and scars on my nose.
When out with the others and put to the test,
I always avowed I would give of my best.

But though I am grizzled and spreading a toe,
My first loving Master, I want you to know,
That when I have done all I can for the pack,
Old Pagan's remembered, one day I'll be back.'

E. A. G. Warlow

Two classes are judged, dogs and bitches, and the puppies are
brought in two by two and encouraged to run across the square
after thrown tidbits. All the hounds come in together for a final
view and then, amidst oohs of disappointment and aahs of
approval, they are one by one eliminated until the winner is
adjudged. Often a champion is decided between the winning dog
and bitch.

A different kind of 'young entry' says hello to an exuberant hound

Roy Tatlow jumping a barbed wire fence

At the end, the judges give a serious talk spiced with risqué jokes, then it is everyone in to the marquee for tea, provided by the ladies of the hunt, with delicious sandwiches, melt-in-the-mouth home-made cakes, scones and strawberries, and gallons of tea, which later on may become whisky. There are silver spoons for all the puppy walkers, engraved with the name of each puppy, and prizes for the best three in each class, as well as a special prize for the 'best entered hound' of the previous year.

The puppies are given names of two syllables that arc easy to be called and begin with the same letter as their mother. If either the sire or dam is from a different pack, that hunt's name is added as a prefix. So, for instance, the champion puppy at the Golden Valley's first puppy show in 1947 was Mabel, whose dam was North Cotswold Mangle; her litter brother, second in the dogs' class, was Marquis, while the winning dog was Linkman, by Brecon Lively. Litter brother Lifeguard was third and, in the bitches, Limit and Lilac were second and third.

Soon a pony show and gymkhana and hunter and sheep dog trials were added to the calendar, as well as a group for making new hunt jumps and clearing rides, a hunt helpers' dinner, an earthstoppers' dinner and a supporters club. Like so many other hunts, it is the backbone of the local country society on all levels.

THE FARMERS' MAN

There's a Man – you must have met him if you ever ride a horse –
Aloof he sits to view our fox a-stealing from the gorse,
He gives him law – then hollers him, and adequately shows
He's good enough to follow him, however straight he goes.

Rancher

How many huntsmen can say, I wonder, that on their retirement day they jumped a full-height barbed wire fence? The picture opposite shows Roy Tatlow doing just that in tremendous style in perfect unison with his horse on his final day hunting the Clifton-on-Teme hounds in 1999. But it is as a 'farmers' man' that he is best remembered. Hunt chairman Francis Lowden summed it up when he said, 'If there were more Roys in this world, hunting wouldn't have any problems.' In Roy's own tribute to the farmers, he spoke of them as 'magic' people over whose land it had been a great privilege to cross. He spoke, too, of the enormous contribution hunting makes to the countryside and of the fellowship it creates.

His was a superb husband-and-wife hunting team, with his wife Mandy working tirelessly behind the scenes and turning the horses out immaculately, and acting as an excellent whipper-in.

The Clifton-on-Teme is a pretty, steeply-sided country in Worcestershire and Herefordshire with much woodland, many lambing ewes and plenty of foxes. There are also several large shoots, but there is a good relationship between the two sports, enabling them to exist hand in hand.

Hunting was a way of life Roy chose as a young man, although he was also a successful amateur jockey and show rider. His youngest brother, David, former multiple point-to-point champion rider and hunter producer and showman of great repute, said simply, 'Roy was my mentor as a child and is one of my three best friends in life.'

Roy rode in the Cheltenham Foxhunters, and won the hunter championship at the Royal Show on Skibereen, but it is for his great rapport with farmers that he is best known in a hunt career that took him through spells at the Monmouthshire, North Cotswold and Albrighton Woodland Hunts, as well as the Clifton-on-Teme.

A traditional marquee tea after a puppy show

X   Ireland

A Toast

Land without rent to you

The women of your choice to you

Days of fine scent to you

And may you die in Ireland

Hounds outside Morrissey's Pub, Laois, Ireland

VISITING

The fiftieth anniversary celebrations for George Briscoe as Master of the Tara Harriers in Co. Meath were a sight to behold. He was a much-admired man and well-wishers attended from far and wide, both for the hunting and for the party held in a huge marquee that night. At first there was no sign of any horses, but they are about the last thing to appear at an Irish lawn meet. The first is the drink, plenty of it. There are also thick black coats with traces of last week's mud on them, and broad Irish brogues, full of friendliness and optimism. After our glasses had been filled again, at last the lorries arrived, and the ancient one carrying the hirelings revealed a motley lot, all travelling loose within it.

'Please don't let mine be the black and white cow, please,' prayed my friend, who was used to riding thoroughbreds in England. Hers was indeed the piebald. A piece of its bridle was held together with twine and the saddle was stiff and worn.

'This is the finest lepper in the whole of Ireland,' she was told, though she didn't look quite reassured. 'Copy the Irish, jump slowly from a trot or even a standstill, and hang on to the neck strap to give the horse's head room to stretch and find that necessary fifth leg. Oh, and whatever else, don't look down,' her friend added, thinking of the first time he had peered down into the seemingly cavernous gorge beyond as he teetered on top of his first bank. The horse could indeed cross the country and gave her a safe ride over the unfamiliar banks and ditches.

Hunting, farming and racing go hand in hand in Ireland. Many farmers breed a horse or two, hunt them, then, as often as not, train them, too. It is a life steeped in tradition and is very

The Galway Blazers, 2001

informal and laid back. As in England, Ireland has its more fashionable packs, notably the Galway Blazers in the west, the Scarteen 'Black and Tans', the Tipperary and the Limerick in the south-west, and the Kildare and the Meath in the East. England's shire hunts will have many provincial and London visitors, while the Irish tend to have many from America, with several becoming Masters.

Tremendous fun can be had, too, in any of the less fashionable hunts. The first day I enjoyed with the Westmeath was typical. At first it appeared that the meet was at the village single-pump petrol station-cum-shop. The flaking shop walls were lined with shelf upon shelf of every imaginable necessity to life. There were wellies and boots and hardware; underwear, socks and shirts; light bulbs, loo paper, groceries, and lovely big,

old-fashioned glass jars full of sweets. Behind the counter, the cheerful assistant weighed out a bag of nails for one customer then, with scarcely a wipe of her hands down her pinnie, began making some sandwiches for another. The floor was bare and there was a slightly beery smell. At the rear was a pair of swing doors. Tentatively I pushed them open – and there was the pub, with the hunt followers in full fluid swing in front of a roaring fire. By the time we emerged to go hunting, all trace of nerves had vanished!

Among the field that day were a young English couple over for them to sample Irish hunting, their first wedding anniversary present to each other. The two lady Masters, Caroline and Dot, had tied the stock for their joint-Master, Martin, and then huntsman James Lowry moved off with the hounds. The

Hounds of the Galway Blazers negotiate a wall in typical Galway country

countryside looks deceptively gentle here; during the day we found ourselves jumping electric wire and brushing through thick thorns. Even in the bright sunshine there was fairly good scent and hounds ran well, giving us some memorable views. Hacking back towards the meet at the end of the day, a wafer-thin moon rose like parchment above a big Georgian house, bordered by drystone walls, and its sheep-dotted grounds sloped to the lake, which reflected the moon. Behind us, a crimson sun set on a memorable day.

THE RYANS AND THE SCARTEEN BLACK AND TANS

The name Ryan is synonymous with the Scarteen hounds. Their country covers much of Counties Limerick and Tipperary in south-west Ireland, renowned for its big banks and ditches, fare for the brave, both horses and riders.

The hounds themselves date back even further and are unique.

When the waters began receding, Noah's Ark, it is said, came to rest on top of Galteemore, Tipperary's highest point. There, a couple of black and tan hounds – one dog, one bitch – scented a fox and leapt off the ark in hot pursuit, never to be seen again. Certainly the hounds, known as Kerry beagles, are 'as old as the hills' and, if not actually from Mesopotamia (present-day Iraq), may in fact have originated in Spain, the result of not infrequent shipwrecks off the rocky coast.

Meeting Thady Ryan, now in his eighties, is one of life's privileges and it is fitting that he entitled his autobiography *A Privileged Life*. Tall, upright and silver-haired, his voice is strong and his eyes sparkle above an aquiline nose, and his long, slender feet are encased in highly polished brown leather shoes. He reminisces about his past and about the famous pack of hounds that have been in the Ryan family at Scarteen, Co. Limerick, for more than 360 years.

He relates the story of how his father, known as Master John, had been buried in a shell-hole, along with a number of others,

LEFT: *Thady Ryan and the Scarteen hounds*
RIGHT: *Thady Ryan at the Opening Meet, November 1994*

Thady Ryan clearing a big bank and ditch, during a fast hunt

during the First World War. German soldiers were coming along to dispatch them, or take them prisoner, one by one. John Ryan was taken to a prisoner-of-war camp where a German officer, who had been hunting in Ireland, recognized him and had him spared. His family and numerous friends in Ireland, having received a telegram of his presumed death, were attending a Mass being said in his memory when a second telegram arrived announcing his rescue. The rug that he was given in the prisoner-of-war camp still hangs in Scarteen. But, for a different reason, John Ryan never forgave the Germans. They treated the prisoners-of-war well, distributed their food parcels and so on, but the way they treated their own recruits upset him. Thady remembers being given, as a child, a lead toy model of a bull; his father saw that it was made in Germany and threw it in the fire.

Thady joined his father in the mastership of the Scarteen hounds in 1946 and carried the horn for the next forty years, during which time he earned as high a reputation as it is possible for a huntsman to have. It included many red-letter days and inevitably, sometimes, anxiety, such as the time the hounds were on a railway track as a train was approaching. The sound of the train muffled Thady's sounds on the horn, the hounds unable to hear his frantic blowing. He feared the worst. The next moment, the kennel huntsman Tommy O'Dwyer trotted up, hounds milling around him. 'All on, sir,' he said.

In August 1986, at the start of the new hunting season, Thady suddenly felt the most excruciating pain in his chest; for two days he lay flat on his back refusing to see a doctor. His son, Chris, recalls, 'It was frightening, and he was getting worse.' Thady was finally taken to hospital, and was given the percentage chances of surviving an operation on his heart. Amazingly, within eight weeks of Thady having chosen to have a double bypass, he was back in the saddle for a half-day's hunting. But poor health meant that he handed over the horn to Chris, his own distinguished career as one of the world's finest huntsmen over.

This marked the dawn of a new era, for he had promised his New Zealand-born wife Anne that when the time came to relinquish the horn, he would take up residency in her native land,

and the couple now live near Christchurch in South Island. 'After all, she had given up thirty years of her home life to be with me, though giving up the horn came a little sooner than I had imagined,' he smiled ruefully.

Hunting in New Zealand cannot compare with Ireland, he says – there are no foxes, for one thing – but Thady is content there, and he can return to his homeland for three months every autumn and winter. He says that in New Zealand 'the hare is not as challenging a quarry species and I don't respect it as much as a fox, who is a magnificent creature. He will keep going, whereas a hare will sit down and get up from under your horse's feet.'

Thady's son, Chris, who has earned an excellent reputation as a huntsman, shows off the thirty-five to forty couple of hounds, a few more bitches than dogs, in the kennels that were newly built at Scarteen in 1994. To help keep them pure but not inbred, the hounds are usually taken for a week's hunting in Co. Kerry, on foot, in March or April, the only piece of country where black and tan hounds are indigenous. From one of the Co. Kerry hounds, a stallion hound is chosen and brought back to Scarteen to infuse fresh blood. Several of the Co. Cork foot packs contain Kerry beagle blood, often mixed with Cavan as a good outcross.

The black and tan hounds are, apart from their colour, renowned for their deep voice, almost as low as that of a blood-

Chris Ryan leads the 'tans' across the Drumcumoge River, January 2001

hound. They are slightly smaller than the average foxhound and have a 'hare' foot (which means that the inside and outside toe are slightly receding, as opposed to the English foxhound's, which are level and thus inclined to be less sound). 'About five of the bloodlines go way back several centuries,' he says proudly, adding, 'we breed about four litters of pups a year.'

Clearly his favourite hound was Highlight, a first cross with an American Penmarydale hound. 'He was second last off a bank when hounds found on one hunt, but he swept through the pack like Nijinsky and caught the fox. Most of our foxes are caught

above ground; we only dig if a farmer asks us to.'

Stories of great hunts and derring-do abound with the Scarteen, and the pack attracts many visitors. 'We could not survive without them,' admits joint-secretary Dick Power. Field-Master Val O'Connor finished third in the Grand National on Yer Man and takes some following across this awesome country. Visitors come in enthusiastic numbers not only from Britain but also from America – some becoming joint-Masters. Even well-known Irishmen from other equestrian disciplines try their hand in the Scarteen country, with varying degrees of success, like the

The four joint-Masters of the Duhallow lead the field. Left to right: David Nagle, Kate Horgan, Maurice O'Connor and Peter Musgrave

occasion when three successful Grand National jockeys came to a high single bank at the back of Scarteen. All three fell, and then a local farrier, Paddy O'Connell, all 20 stone of him, coat flapping open, popped his grey hunter up and off the bank. An eighty-four-year-old American lady rider was also jumping successfully when she heard that her younger friend had fallen. 'Can't do anything about that,' she replied, 'hounds are running.' And on she continued.

A familiar irritation for a huntsman is to find he is being 'tailgated' by over-enthusiastic 'thrusters', to the detriment of his work with the hounds, who like to be left in peace to seek out a line. Dick Power remembers one such occasion when the huntsman called back, 'This one's big!' There was a canal dead ahead on the landing side, unseen by the follower but known to the huntsman, who therefore turned his horse at a right-angle on to the towpath immediately on landing. 'He didn't bother to look round; instead he just listened to the splash as the visiting rider fell into the canal.' Another intrepid follower, one Chris Lorseman riding a nutty grey horse, was seen to jump from a trot four strands of barbed wire stretched taught between two narrow concrete posts. No one else attempted the feat.

The only time in its history that there hasn't been a Ryan at the Scarteen helm was in the 1930s when the family was in financial trouble for nearly a decade following the failure of Sadlers Bank in which they had invested.

For the 2002–2003 season, unusually in hunting circles, there were no fewer than seven joint-Masters, hailing from four countries: Chris Ryan, Semon Wolf (formerly from Wall Street, USA) and John Edwards from Ireland, the latter two having both been in the mastership since 1982, along with American politician William 'Bill' Hobby from Texas. The other Masters are Ian Hurst from South Africa; English farmer Roger Dungworth, who is also a joint-Master of the Cottesmore; and, of course, Thady Ryan from New Zealand.

As a farmers' pack, injection of funds from outside sources has always been welcomed, although these days it is secure enough to raise money on occasion for non-hunting causes. One such example was when a child was sent from Limerick to America for treatment for a tumour. It is a far cry from the penal period of the late 1700s to early 1800s when to be Catholic would mean, for instance, that any horse worth more than £5 would be confiscated.

THE OLDEST HUNT

THE STEEPLE

Our forbears saw the Steeple
Stand bold against the Blue,
A landmark to the people
Who sought for porch and pew;
And while the tall spire bade them
To prayer and praise withdraw,
How it might further aid them
Our sporting fathers saw.

So when men matched their horses
To gallop fast and far,
Before the days of courses
Built up with birch and bar,
That needle-cloud embordered
Our fathers chose for guide,
And dropped the flag and ordered:
'Straight for the Steeple – ride!'

Now, o'er the hamlet houses
We watch the lifted spire,
And in each heart it rouses
Some old and smouldering fire;
And many cheery people,
Though far removed from grace,
Look kindly on the Steeple,
That gave the Steeple-chase.

Will Ogilvie

An early bath is taken whilst out hunting for the Duhallow!

The Duhallow is Ireland's oldest pack of hounds, dating from some time before 1745, and is therefore steeped in history. It was also home to the first recorded steeplechase in 1752 from Buttevant to Doneraile between two hunting men, Edmund Blake and Cornelius O'Callaghan, and since then it has spawned some of the world's finest National Hunt jockeys, notably Jonjo O'Neill. He learnt to ride with the dashing Duhallows and those who remembered him then were not so surprised by the awe-inspiring ride he gave Dawn Run to win the Cheltenham Gold Cup in 1986.

The Duhallow country covers a large tract of Co. Cork, and is wild and hairy. The pack was owned and hunted first by one Henry Wrixham of Ballygiblin, then his son, Colonel William Wrixham and in turn by his son, Sir William Wrixham Becher. In 1822, the latter gave the hounds to the hunt, when his brother-in-law, Robert de la Cour, took over the mastership until 1849.

During the 1950s one of the joint-Masters was Harry Freeman Jackson, one of Ireland's finest horsemen, while at the helm since 1986 has been Mrs Kate Horgan.

A ONE-MAN BAND

Many Irish harrier packs hunt fox, or fox and hare; comparatively few hunt only hare. The sporting Killinick Harriers in Co. Wexford, founded in 1886, have hunted fox only in living memory. Traditionally a one-man band, the hunt is just about the first stop from the Rosslare ferry from Wales. Longevity is a byword, which is just as well, for it is customary for the incumbent Master to kennel and look after the hounds. He will also hunt them, visit the farmers, pick up the flesh and organize just about everything else in the day-to-day running of the hunt.

The pack was bought originally in 1886 by Mr P. Doran and since then there have been only five Masters. James Davis hunted them for twenty seasons, Paddy Codd for twenty-two, Jack Deacon for four years in the 1960s, and then Matt Roche was another of twenty-two years until 1989. Since then, the man at the helm has been John Stafford, a neat, dapper farmer who

John Stafford

converted pigsties on his farm at Dennistown near Wexford to kennel the hounds.

It is from the backs of his point-to-pointers or his coloured stallions that he frequently hunts the hounds. The hounds mainly have black and tan ancestry, infused successfully in modern times with Galway and Beaufort blood; only a few of the true harrier type remain.

John Stafford was eight years old when he started hunting on a snow-white working farm cob called Paddy, his interest having been kindled by an uncle who was also a priest. He remembers one particular hunt when Matt Roche was hunting the hounds. About forty people were out when a fox was found at Harvestown. 'Hounds ran and ran and ran non-stop for $2^1/2$ hours and the horses were nearly unconscious,' he remembers. Only six riders were up at the finish, and they dismounted and walked their horses home.

Another keen member of the hunt was Tuppence the terrier. He was bought to be a pet for John and Breda Stafford's elder daughter Katie, but soon he started hunting with the pack, and became recognized all over Co. Wexford. At first he just joined in on hound exercise; then one day he managed to slip in unnoticed on a hunting day. He became accepted, and was particularly useful in thick cover. Inevitably, he sometimes got left behind, but he was either picked up by a car follower or, on occasion, sat on the front of a rider's saddle. Sadly, he disappeared one day out hunting and was never found.

John Stafford has an unorthodox way of training puppies to hunt, too. 'They are born in the sheds, and when she is ready to, the mother simply takes them off hunting round the farm and they learn naturally.' It is all part of the laid-back way of life, to which visitors are always welcomed.

XI   New Zealand

Beagles were brought to the Auckland
area of New Zealand by Governor Sir
George Grey in 1868. The Pakuranga
Hunt was formed in 1873, followed by
the Christchurch in 1880. From the
start, the packs were well regulated.
Heat and hard ground prevent hunting
starting before the end of March or
early April, and it continues until July
when lambing gets under way.

The placid beauty of Karaka, North Island, New Zealand

All New Zealand's mammals were originally imported from England, including the hare that is the quarry species. There are no foxes; the story goes that a dog fox and vixen were found in a crate on a ship and promptly dropped into the bottom of the harbour.

In July 2002, I travelled across the world to New Zealand for some hunting Down Under. When I landed on the North Island, water lay in pools at the roadside, rivers were flooded, paddocks waterlogged. Worse, hunting was cancelled. 'We've had more rain than anyone can ever remember. In the last six weeks the longest period without rain has been twenty-one hours.' It sounded a familiar story to English ears.

PAKURANGA

My first port of call was to New Zealand's oldest hunt, the Pakuranga, which is also closest to the premier city, Auckland, whose growing population has spread over the site of its original kennels at Pigeon Mountain. The kennels now are at Karaka,

Ross Coles, Pakuranga

and there I was to 'show my paces' jumping a strange horse over wire under the watchful gaze of huntsman and former international show-jumper Ross Coles prior to hunting the next day.

It is normal practice for New Zealanders to jump wire, but it puts the fear up visitors. The important thing to remember is that most of the horses know nothing else and jumping it is as second nature to them as banks and ditches are to an Irish horse. The wire is prepared in many areas much like an English hunt jump, slightly cut down and with the supporting batten tops painted white. The battens are so close together in some areas that they resemble chestnut paling fences. It was still raining and it continued so hard throughout the night that hunting the next day was cancelled. Instead, we rode 10 miles along the beach to the mouth of the Waikato River and back, a glorious exercise, but no hounds and not the same as hunting.

It gave me a chance to talk to Ross Coles, a man who made a success of following in his well-known father's footsteps, the two of them having hunted these hounds for an amazing fifty consecutive seasons, with Ross taking over in 1983. He reckons to jump some 5,000 fences per season, or getting on for 100,000 in twenty years. 'Yes, we're a jumping hunt,' he grins, adding that he will often jump full-height, unprepared wire in order to keep with hounds.

Their season starts at Easter and traditionally there are thirty-eight meets per season (fewer than in Britain), ending in the first week of August. That is followed a week later by the annual point-to-point which, besides races for thoroughbreds over fences, also has races for juniors, flat races and races open to 'hairy horses'.

When Ross's father, Ray, became a professional whip to the Pakuranga, under Englishman P. H. 'Val' Smith, who had been huntsman since the 1920s, he would have to sit in the truck at the end of the day while Val and the Master went into their host's house for drinks, but there is no sense of 'them and us' now.

Throughout his time there, Ray Coles always showed dedication and consideration to breeding for type and built up a legendary reputation as a sportsman. He would be a hard act for any young man to follow. His youngest son, Graeme, was being groomed for the role, but tragically was killed just a month after the wedding of middle brother Ross. The consequent lifestyle turning point saw Ross quit the office job he had had since leaving school, but it was not too difficult a decision. He had been hunting since he was nine and, like his two brothers (the other, Alan, is head stipendary of Auckland Racing District), he was an amateur whip. So it was a natural progression and, although not easy to follow such a fine man, he was not fazed by it. 'I just got on with the job and Father always encouraged me.'

Ross had raced as an amateur jockey as well as represented New Zealand as a show-jumper and been short-listed for the Olympic Games. He is also clerk of the course at Ellerslie racecourse, which is not a desk job but that of an outrider, escorting runners to the start, catching loose horses and so on, and a traditional role of the local huntsman.

Ross is proud of New Zealand's horses and riders. 'They are natural across country and we have an endless supply of thoroughbreds, many of whom have gone on to be world superstars.'

He is proud of his hounds, which in 2002 numbered nineteen couple with six couple of puppies, much influenced by English blood, especially the Cambridgeshire Harriers and also the High Peak and the Pendle Forest and Craven. 'I'm very fussy about size,' Ross explained, 'I try to keep them to the true harrier size of under 21 inches [at the shoulder], but the most important thing is to breed them for their hunting ability.'

TAUPO

Two more hunts were cancelled for the next day, but thankfully the Taupo was on, so my delightful hostess, Sarah Milne, along with the huntsman of the cancelled Waikato Hunt, Lauryn Robertson, and I set off on the 2 1/2-hour lorry drive.

As good fortune would have it, the day was my only dry one, the sun was out and, as we drove along the shores of North Island's largest lake, Lake Taupo, the water sparkled. We journeyed on until we reached New Zealand's National Equestrian Centre, where the meet was held. The old grass here was dotted with event fences, tempting for several riders to jump. Hounds were busy all day for huntsman Tim Wellwood, with several short runs. I was impressed with the overall standard of horses and riding, and saw very few refusals or falls at the wire fences. One run took us into the heathland at one end of a geothermal lake, where we were careful to keep to the tracks, for the soggy surrounding soil was full of geyser springs bubbling with boiling water. And the stench of the sulphur! It was a wonder the hounds could hunt at all.

The meet was at 12 and pack-up time was 3 p.m., more or less regardless, but at least everyone stays out for the full time. Then there was the hunt tea, all part of the tradition in both New Zealand and Australia. First we washed off, loaded and fed the horses. As usual, I then pulled off my boots and began unfastening my stock, when Sarah advised, 'You'll have to put them on again for the tea.' It was full fig, and smart for it. Everybody brings along a contribution to the tea, pooling it on the long table, and no one starts to eat until the Master, in this case Andrew Bremner, begins. At the end, the Master gave a speech and thanked the landowners, then asked me to give the assembled company news of hunting in England and the work of the Countryside Alliance. Afterwards, they all filled in the 'marching in spirit' form. It was a good, enjoyable day with the people as friendly and as hospitable as they are anywhere in the hunting world – one of the many reasons why I love it so much. On the way home, a crowd of us had an amusing and memorable evening at the Loose Goose.

'WORKING UP' – AND HOW!

A SINGLE HOUND

The huntsman had gathered his pack and gone;
The last late hoof had echoed away;
The horn was twanging a long way on
For the only hound that was still astray.

Will Ogilvie

Although the Taupo was my only official day, I had an exhilarating, unofficial hunt elsewhere during my stay, one that was strictly 'off the record' and shall, therefore, remain nameless. I was invited to join the huntsman and whipper-in in 'working up' the hounds on a farm (or property, as most farms are known in New Zealand unless they are big enough to be a station). It was too wet to have any followers, we would be out for a couple of hours, and there would be strictly no jumping. 'We'll just be cautiously slipping our way across the fields, and giving the hounds a bit of practice,' I was told.

For the first 1 1/2 hours we found no fresh hares, just a bit of stale drag every now and again, and I was impressed with the hounds' obedience each time the huntsman called them back to him. The country was beautiful, very steep, with one or two copses in the combs and on the hilltops.

'There's one more place to try, and I guarantee we'll have found within five minutes,' the huntsman gave the familiar assurance, only sometimes correct, to waiting followers' ears. It was now nearly 1 p.m., our planned packing-up time. About four minutes later, a big hare got up right in front of the pack of hounds. Immediately, they were in full cry. Equally quickly we set off in hot pursuit and as the first fence, a hedge, came and went, all notions of no jumping were dispelled.

'Don't worry, you're on one of the best jumpers in New Zealand,' the whipper-in called back as we approached a full-height set of wire, neither cut down nor painted white. Hounds were already well ahead of us, running at great pace; our adrenalin was up, our only object to keep with them. We turned towards another big, upright fence – no time to stop and open the gate – and sped on up the hill, jumped another set of wire, over the hilltop, and the hounds were completely out of sight on neighbouring property, from whose owner permission had not been sought for hunting.

But we could hear them, hunting fast and in full cry – and heading for a large tract of bush of several hundred acres. We had to try to stop them, but now we were confronted by boundary wire topped by electric fence with the ground dropping away to a steep gulley on the other side. Not even the intrepid pair I was with could attempt to jump that. The whip went off in one direction, the huntsman in another, looking for ways to get round to the hounds, while I stayed put, keeping with me the one hound that had returned.

Soon both riders were out of sight, and all I had was the vast view of the surrounding countryside, the enormous wood and the sound, emanating from deep within it, of the pack of hounds. Very often, hounds will check and there will be silence while they try to recover the scent, but not this time. Their music was non-stop, echoing from the bush. Occasionally birds rose in front of them, and once or twice sheep in the distant pasture moved hastily as one or two hounds emerged, only to return to the depths of the bush.

My two companions returned, the whip with another couple of hounds, the huntsman bereft. Now the rain began to fall, mist was closing in, and the huntsman blew in vain upon his horn. It was not that the hounds were being disobedient but that they were hunting so hard and we were so far away from them that they couldn't hear our calls. I began to imagine them being there for three days, so dense was it.

Next the horses were abandoned – I held on to all three, with about two couple of hounds – while the whip and the huntsman climbed the barbed wire and set off into the bush. There were no paths and the undergrowth was so thick that they made little progress. The sound of hounds, which had swung this way and that for 2 hours, was fading further into the distance. We would just have to see how far round the edge of the wood we could get, taking the few hounds with us. The poor whip was due to give a riding lesson at 4 p.m., and we were a long way from the lorry and then a good half-hour drive home. She had also organized a number of friends to come to dinner for me to meet.

Eventually, the huntsman told us to go back when the time came, and he disappeared into the depths again on foot. We had no alternative but to do as he said, and tie his horse to the fence while we set off with our 'pack' – by now totalling three and a half couple – and try to retrace our steps up hill and down dale,

Jumping a typical wire fence with the Taupo hunt

all of it looking different in the mist. After the lesson, held in pouring rain, the whip received a call from the huntsman saying he had picked up all the hounds bar one, and had put them in a friendly farmer's barn, but he didn't know where his horse was.

With cooking instructions quickly passed on to an incredibly tolerant husband – one suspected it wasn't an entirely novel scenario for him – the whip dashed off to the rescue in the car and borrowed a quad bike to get across the terrain now in total darkness. She found the horse still tied to the fence, and the one remaining hound waiting patiently beside him. Later that evening, the huntsman arrived at the party barefoot. Both his heels were skinned raw in circles the size of a large coin, rubbed by his boots as he traipsed through the bush.

More storms followed my route south. This time snow and sleet intermingled with the constant horizontal rain in the raging gales. It was too rough for the ferry to cross the Cook Straits and so, with real regret, I abandoned my proposed hunting in the South Island and headed for sunnier climes. It was wonderful to feel the sheer warmth that greeted me as I emerged from the plane at 11 p.m. in Fiji. In only 3 ½ hours I had gone from 4 to 24°C, and it was bliss.

I soon discovered there is some hunting in Fiji, strictly illegal. The trekking guide, who was escorting double his usual number with two of us, told us that the cur dogs we saw in some of the remote villages were gathered together at night and used to hunt wild pigs, which were then killed with spears. Cloak-and-dagger stuff, but better than the cannibalism that was still practised only 150 years ago until the coming of the Christian missionaries.

XII Australia

The land to the south of the Victorian

Alps in Australia is called the High

Country, famous for its portrayal in

The Man from Snowy River, infamous

for the exploits of bushranger and

outlaw Ned Kelly. Here, the stations

cover hundreds of square miles, the

bush thousands. The visitor is greeted

laughingly by the kookaburras and

noisily by the magpies.

Colin Reynolds at his retirement meet with the Munsfield

IN THE HIGH COUNTRY

The silver-grey and olive-green of the eucalyptus is brightened by the red rosellas, the pink and grey galah parrots, the mimicking lyrebirds with their peacock-style tails, the white and the black cockatoos, the red and green king parrots, the wedge-tailed eagles and the scarlet robins.

Elsewhere, the stumps are blackened, the ground scorched, a grim reminder of the tinder-like qualities of this semi-tamed land. It is a country of free-roaming kangaroos and wallabies sharing the coarse grazing with the sheep and cattle. And it is a country of foxes.

I am in northern Victoria, just below the Victorian Alps, home to one of Australia's smaller hunts, the Mansfield. The Mansfield borrows the hounds of its neighbouring pack, the Yarra Glen and Lilydale, on the eight Sundays of the year on which it meets. On the positive side, members are allowed to hunt with both packs. The Mansfield Hunt is in the well-foxed country centred around

Hunting in Australia among the eucalypti.

Mansfield and Merrijig. Merrijig is best known as a ski centre for Mount Buller, in the Australian Alps, and for being the nearest township to Timbertop, the Outward Bound-style branch of Australia's famous Geelong Grammar School.

Its original settlers in the 1860s were nearly all Irish – the Purcells, Hearns, Mahoneys, keen hunting men all – and they did not take long in establishing a pack of hounds on what was known as the Devil's Plain. The hotel in Merrijig bears the name the Hunt Club Hotel and hounds were hunting along the Devil's River at the turn of the last century. The hunt then lapsed until an attempt was made to reform it after the Second World War. When the mastermind behind it, Bob Coombs, died on what was to have been its reopening morning, the club died with him.

It was not re-formed until 1980, when one dog hound and four bitches were purchased from the Oaklands Hunt Club by Jim Taylor. He formed a private pack to hunt on the Star Glen Ranch at Bonnie Doon, more hounds were purchased and John Kavanagh was employed by the ranch to hunt the pack. When Jim Taylor left the area, he gave the pack to John Kavanagh. The following year, the hunt was opened to more people; it was named the Devil's River Hunt and Dr Rod Graham, a vet and a great character, was the popular founding Master.

More recently, it was renamed the Mansfield Hunt Club and became a member of the official Association of Hunt Clubs. Sharing the mastership with Rod Graham for a number of seasons was Colin Reynolds, a former jackaroo, show-pony rider and dairy farmer. His relatively late start in hunting began with the Melbourne Hunt Club whose Master, Sir Alex Creswick, was also chairman of the Victoria Racing Club, Flemington, venue of the world-famous Melbourne Cup every November. He recalls, 'Rod Graham bred up a pack of ten to twelve couple, I kept half at home and another farmer had the other half; we got together to exercise them during the week. We had some puppies bred from English stallion hounds from the Melbourne and Oakland hunts – people are very generous. Hounds work regularly and they work pretty damn well. Smaller clubs like us all take a pride in our hounds and our hunt.'

When Colin's wife became ill and then died, he had to give up and people came from all around for his retirement meet. One of the features he inaugurated was the annual children's meet and another is the practice at many meets of catering for a non-jumping field with its own separate field-Master.

In the 1990s, the hunt formed its arrangement with the Yarra Glen, using their hounds and huntsman, but retaining their own Master, who is Michael O'Dea. It is a small hunt following the best of traditions, including refusing to die.

Australia has just over twenty Hunt Clubs, as they are known, mostly in Victoria but also South Australia, Western Australia, New South Wales and a couple in Tasmania. They adhere rigidly to the customs and traditions of English hunting dress and etiquette, no matter how hot it may be. They have added touches of their own, though, notably the hunt breakfast held at the conclusion of each day.

AUSTRALIA'S LEICESTERSHIRE

The pack with the highest reputation is the Ellerslie Camperdown, based in a lovely area south-west of Melbourne near Camperdown, close to the surf for those who prefer sea sport. The pack is maintained avidly by John Crosbie Goold who re-formed the pack in 1983, the original 1860s pack having been closed down since the Second World War. He has earned a reputation as an excellent huntsman and sagacious hound breeder, frequently taking the advice of Captain Brian Fanshawe in England. He also acknowledges the first-class assistance he receives from the staff in the hunting field and in the modern kennels that he has built.

It is a hunt country of wide open territory dotted by a few lone volcanic cones and a scattering of trees, of bubbling rivers winding their way through cattle pastures and sheep stations enclosed by wire and with panel fences placed strategically as hunt jumps – and foxes everywhere. 'They breed like rabbits,' I was told, 'and the farmers are only too happy to have the hunt.' The views stretch as far as the eye can see, perfect for viewing foxes away, for watching hounds hunt them, and for riding the best and the fittest of thoroughbreds to keep up with them, for the runs are long, frequent, and fast. Look out Leicestershire!

XIII The United States

Hunting in America is as old as the country itself, the first settlers having been required to take one dog each to help hunt for food, as well as to act as guard dogs. Once they began to gain a little free time, it did not take long for them to arrange some more organized hunting. In 1650, Robert Brooke landed to take up his appointment from Lord Baltimore as Privy Council of State for the province of Maryland, bringing with him his wife, ten children, twenty-eight servants, and a pack of hounds.

The Blue Ridge Hounds crossing a creek in Virginia

Over a stone wall in Piedmont country, Virginia

FOLLOWING TRADITION

George Washington was a keen foxhunter, having learnt much as a sixteen-year-old from Lord Fairfax who had established one of the earliest packs in Virginia, now hunted over by the Blue Ridge Hounds. Washington founded his own pack in 1767 and hunted until the outbreak of the American Revolution (1775–83). He led his countrymen to victory against the British and became the United States' first President in 1789, but he restarted his hounds after the war and kept copious hunting journals. Perhaps it is no coincidence that on retirement as President after two terms in office he was admired for his qualities of leadership, stoicism and integrity – all qualities abundant in the hunting field.

These early packs were informal, private affairs. The first recognized packs of hounds were the Montreal Hunt in Canada in 1826, followed by the Piedmont, Virginia, in 1840, and the Rose Tree Hunt Club, Pennsylvania, in 1859. The American Masters of Foxhounds Association was founded in 1907, its aims to preserve the quality of the sport, to encourage new hunts and Masters, and to produce the hound Stud Book.

The sport is thriving in America and its followers offer vocal and practical support to the cause for keeping hunting going in Britain. Some 400 individual Americans journeyed to London for the big march in 2002. Hunting takes place in many of the eastern States, including Virginia (whose Piedmont district became known as the Leicestershire of America), Maryland, Kentucky, the Carolinas, even Florida, as well as the great plains of the Midwest, the Rocky Mountains and California on the western seaboard. The quarry is nearly as varied as the terrain: traditional red fox in New England, Virginia, Maryland,

Pennsylvania and Delaware; in the Deep South of Alabama, Georgia and the Carolinas, coyote and bobcat will be hunted through the pine woods, as well as red and grey fox; the palm trees of Florida see fox and coyote hunting, while the sand-dunes of Long Island are home to red fox. Going further west, the coyote is a big, fast, wide-ranging quarry that carries a strong scent. Over the years a number of English huntsmen have left their legacy in the States, while several Americans have become Masters on this side of the Atlantic, particularly in Ireland.

In an autumn of the early 1980s, during a heatwave, I found myself mounted at 6 a.m. for a meet of the Green Spring Valley Hounds, Maryland, and already the temperature was 22°C. America is prone to extremes of temperature. The riders in red coats were sweltering; Americans are great traditionalists, especially in their hunting. The ground was hard, the scent poor, the heat intense, but the fraternity, as always among hunting Americans, was excellent, and the welcome given to a visitor was as warm as the sun.

It was during this visit to the States that, apart from enjoying some very warm mornings' hunting with the Elkridge Harper and Green Spring Valley Hunts, I also visited a typical kennel. This was the Red Mountain in North Carolina, whose Yorkshire incumbent, Fred Cockerill, had done so much in sixteen years to build up the then infant pack that he and his wife, affectionately known as 'Mr and Mrs Fred', were held in high esteem throughout the country. It was the inherent

Hunting with the Glenmore, Virginia, in the snow

OVERLEAF: *The Live Oak Hounds of Florida, with masters and staff*

Hunting in Santa Fe – a Californian whipper-in in action jumping over a typical coop

friendliness of Americans that turned the couple's one-year visit into a couple of decades. 'They are so genuine, and have all the time in the world for you,' Fred said.

Fred built up the pack using an Eridge hound, Wiseman, given to him by Major Bob Field-Marsham, as well as Wynnstay and Beaufort blood. By the time the pack was accepted for registration by the Masters of Foxhounds of America in 1980, Fred lost no time in showing and winning with some of his hounds. I particularly remember the spotless cleanliness of the kennels, despite just one man looking after twenty-five or so couple of hounds.

The hunting days are generally short, mainly because about three hours is enough for most of the followers, and the fences are mostly 'chicken coops' over wire; where there is much woodland, trails are cut through. There is a strong social scene associated with the hunting and 'antis' are virtually unheard of, because, I was told, so few foxes are killed. In fact, hunting is not considered a blood sport in America because the object is the chase rather than the kill.

OF RATTLESNAKES AND MOUNTAIN LIONS

Most of the eastern seaboard hunting strongly follows British traditions; while etiquette and dress is also observed further west, the hunting itself is not the same at all, as I heard from Englishman Stephen Petitt. He hunted with the Tedworth for twenty seasons and various other English packs, but has now found himself whipping in to the High Country Coyote pack in Flagstaff,

Arizona. He and his wife moved to Phoenix, Arizona, in September 2000 for nine months but, three years on, they look like staying.

When I asked him to describe the hunting there, I didn't really expect to hear about rattlesnakes, mountain lions or bows and arrows. He told me, 'Flagstaff is at 5,500 feet with high, open plains on volcanic sand and rock interspersed with juniper trees; nearer to Flagstaff some territory is quite alpine in amongst large pines.

'The last two seasons I have whipped in with the Paradise Valley Beagles, whose Master and huntsman is Suzi Stephenson. They hunt the jack rabbit (a lightweight fast hare), and are based in Phoenix.

'The season usually closes early April or at the appearance of the first rattlesnakes – really! Terrain is hazardous, sharp granite rock, saguaro, chain, compass barrel and jumping cholla cacti. (The latter necessitates one carrying forceps to remove the spines which are very difficult to take out.) Compass barrel cactus spines always cause infection. There are also agave plants which are like steel tipped daggers; nearly all the foliage has barbs or spines.'

There is almost zero humidity, making scenting difficult, but, he says, the hard-working beagles usually manage a good chase and occasional kill. Coyote, short of finding a suicidal one, are nearly uncatchable, because they run at up to 40mph and they can operate cleverly as a pack.

Stephen has hunted with the Juan Thomas Coyote Hounds in New Mexico, where huntsman Juan Thomas confirmed they are rarely caught, though he 'has a damn fine try' to do so. He also retains a couple of hounds on his 34,000-acre ranch exclusively to hunt mountain lion, which his sons usually kill with a bow and arrow.

'Believe me, they are a wild bunch,' Stephen said. 'I have seen the trophies all around their house and they look scary enough on the wall, let alone being within a few yards of them when they are shot. 'They really are a great family, and live 40-odd miles up a dirt track with Apache Indians for neighbours.'

Yet even out there, the hunt etiquette and dress code is similar to that in England, although slightly less formal. 'Here it is acceptable to dress and hunt western style to encourage the cowboys to come out. Yes, we really have them here!'

XIV Beagling and Mink Hunting

Traditionally, horsemen follow harriers, while the smaller beagles are hunted from on foot, with the hare being the mutual quarry. In Britain today, the remaining harrier packs often hunt the fox. It is different in New Zealand, where there are no foxes and so hares are the exclusive quarry of the twenty-nine harrier packs.

David and Sarah Manning.
David is also a joint-Master of the Cottesmore

BEAGLING

When the Association of Masters of Harriers and Beagles was founded in 1891, there were 107 packs of harriers and forty of beagles recognized. Today, there are seventy-four packs of beagles recognized in England, which include three American packs: the Nantucket–Treweryn in Virginia, the Paradise Valley in Arizona and the Woodfield in Florida. Now there are just twenty-one harrier packs, including those that hunt the fox exclusively, such as the Cotley; twenty-five packs of beagles are registered in Ireland. There are also eleven packs of basset hounds registered with the Masters of Basset Hounds Association, including one from France, the Rallye Beauvautrait, and one from America, the Skycastle.

Many privately owned harrier packs connected to large estates had either folded or switched exclusively to fox by the late 1800s. Packs of beagles have nearly doubled in that time and, while many are supported by lifelong devotees, there are a number whose role it is to bring on the 'young entry'.

THE BOY BEAGLERS (AND GIRLS)

In October 1952, thirteen-year-old schoolboy Rob 'Buzz' Watts attended the inaugural meet of the Marlborough College Beagles. The pack's formation had been the ambition of Martin Letts, who had left the previous summer, and founding Masters James Bouskell, who had stayed on to turn dream into reality, and Nicholas Wykes. In the eyes of Rob Watts, they were already grown men, way out of his league. Martin Letts became one of the country's best-known huntsmen and has been at the helm of the College Valley and North Northumberland since 1964 (see pp. 82–3).

Rob Watts became a Master of the Marlborough College Beagles, but when he left school it was the world of film production that lured him to California to work on three *Indiana Jones* and another three *Star Wars* films. When he attended the fiftieth anniversary meet of the Marlborough College Beagles on 5 October 2002, it was his first sight of any hounds in forty-six years.

'Here I was standing in Court and I realized the last time had been in March 1956, when I hunted hounds for the last time. Maybe it is because I had experienced the ultimate trip, at the age of seventeen, of hunting hounds myself, that I have never hunted since, but maybe it is because I had a burning desire to go into films that I ceased to hunt and became a film producer instead. Certainly my visit to the fiftieth anniversary was nostalgic.'

The anniversary meet brought a sparkling Indian summer day as, with Marlborough's Mop Fair in full swing down its renowned wide High Street, the hounds were boxed up to Marlborough Downs. There, with rolling views in every direction and plenty of hares, the incumbent Huntsman, Henry Dowty, showed, at fifteen years of age, that he has what it takes to hunt hounds. Kennel huntsman Michael 'Ossie' Osman went further, declaring, 'He has an affinity with hounds to die for.'

Also in the field was Timothy Main, who twenty years before had been hunting the hounds on the occasion of the pack's thirtieth anniversary. A hare was put up immediately at Old Eagle and ran straight out over the racecourse gallops. Hounds ran well on the old turf, but once on plough the scent was scanty. Nevertheless, enough was done for the tea at Michael Osman's flat to be especially welcome; it was laid on by joint-Master Tom Blanchard's parents, Pam and Peter.

Four schools run packs: Eton, Marlborough, Radley and Stowe. Some of their youthful Masters have gone on to be well-known Masters of Foxhounds, headed by Ronnie Wallace. Most of these packs have an adult kennel huntsman at their helm to guide the young Masters, to look after the hounds during the school holidays and to provide a constant factor in the hounds' lives, for the school pupils are unlikely to be involved for more than a year or two. Two such men are John Fretwell of the Stowe Beagles, founder of the Union of Country Sports Workers, and Michael Osman, who achieved a life's ambition of coming into hunt service once he had retired in his fifties from his trade of plumber. The Union of Country Sports Workers was launched in April 1997 with the aim to 'protect the livelihoods of those who are employed in country sports and related

Joint-Masters of the Marlborough College Beagles: Tom Blanchard, Henry Dowty (Huntsman), James Boggis and Charlie Talbot Baker (kneeling), with follower Verity Clarke

businesses whose jobs would be threatened by legislation against fieldsports.'

From a non-hunting family, Michael Osman's ambition of entering hunt service was formed when he was taken hunting by a friend in the Lake District. 'The village school I went to in Ambleside has fifteen past and present hunt staff,' he says proudly. His early ambition was thwarted by his mother, who had arranged for a plumbing apprenticeship, but he continued to follow the fell hounds as often as possible. All those years

later, he came south to be kennelman–terrierman at the Old Berks, before taking up the Marlborough appointment. One does not even have to ask him if he's glad he made such a career change so late in life: his face says it all.

Michael Osman sees his role as one of guiding the youngsters, but confesses, 'Sometimes I feel the hounds are easier to control than the pupils!' He likes to explain which dog hound he is using for breeding and why, and to instruct generally in the role of running a kennel and hunting a pack. Old friend John

Fretwell gives him advice on breeding, helping him to build up a quality pack. 'I just want hounds that hunt well, that's more important than showing, but conformation is important and if they've got quality they'll last longer.'

On average about twelve pupils follow the beagles, and only once has Michael Osman lost one. There was a very high wind and pouring rain; they packed up early and headed off for tea while Ossie went searching for the pupil. He found him, trudging along in the plough towards home, having been unable to hear anything in the gale. 'The boys make lifelong friends beagling,' says Michael Osman, 'and for some lads at the "grunt" stage it brings them out and gives them confidence.'

AN IRISH WELCOME

I got a warm welcome on my first visit to an Irish pack of beagles, including hot whiskey in the home of retired farmer Brian Lovely and his generous wife Marie, over whose land we would principally be hunting. There was only a handful of people present, including three of the joint-Masters, one of whom, Sam Norton, was responsible for founding the hunt, the Westmeath Foot Beagles, in 1999 when he was only ten years old. He persuaded his father, James Norton, former Press Relations Officer of the Irish Masters of Foxhounds Association and a founder of the Hunting Association of Ireland, to hunt them.

Warmed inwardly, we piled on extra clothing to brave the cold outside, all bar Joe Fitzsimmons, who, to my astonishment, was stripping down to short shirtsleeves. We soon saw why, for this fifty-ish joint-Master ran the feet off the rest of us. Only Sam and ten-year-old Thomas Maxwell were a match and the three of them are able whippers-in to joint-Master and huntsman James Norton.

With the encouragement of lifelong beaglers Paul and Mary Stephenson from Rhode, Co. Offaly, James and Sam have built up a private pack of twenty-five couple with drafts principally

The Stowe Beagles with their huntsman Mark Ollard and whipper-in Guy Pelly

The Westmeath Foot Beagles

from the Eton College kennels. The Stephensons introduced Joe Fitzsimmons to the pack and a firm bond was made between him and the Master–huntsman, opening much of north Westmeath to the beagles. The mastership quartet is completed by the affable Robert Dore, a 'strategic' follower who is an expert at placing himself on the nearest high vantage point from which to watch the hounds and the rest of us running round below.

What struck me most, apart from the obvious rapport between Master and whips – a glance here, a hand signal there – was the way James Norton had his small pack so well up together. Their obedience to him, coupled with their enthusiasm for hunting and their excellent voice, was pure pleasure to witness, something subsequent visits showed to be no fluke. The countryside is beautiful and gives excellent viewing from on foot, the band of followers are keen and the pack is a fine example of how hunting can be just as enjoyable on a small scale.

MINK HUNTING

Mink-hunting is generally a gentle day out for the followers, meandering along a stream or riverbank, admiring the hounds' adroitness in water, and just occasionally exerting oneself to run. But there is nothing gentle about the prey, for the mink is a vicious killer.

Mink was farmed for its fur in America, and the 1920s saw the first imports to farms in Britain, where some escaped into the wild. Then misguided animal rights activists purposefully released many from mink farm cages, and they have caused untold damage to the wildlife of river stretches: kingfishers, mallard, moorhens, water voles, all have suffered and in some places have been exterminated by mink.

Mink made a 'natural' alternative to otter hunting when, in the mid-1970s, otter huntsmen alerted river authorities to the plight of the otter, its numbers falling drastically because of pollution, water extraction, bank clearance and river straightening. The ignorance of the 'men in grey suits' in authorizing such action, resulting in rivers running in straight lines, denuded of natural vegetation growing at its edges, is mind-boggling, and illustrates that it is not only the 'antis' who are misguided. Nowadays, curves are being put back into rivers and reed beds reinstated, not only to help the wildlife habitat but also to help prevent flooding. It is an example of why the running of the countryside should be left to those who understand nature and who have been born and bred to country life. There are twenty-four registered packs of mink hounds in the United Kingdom,

and two in Co. Cork, Ireland. Some of them switched directly from otter to mink, such as the Culmstock in Devon, which dates from 1790, and the Ytene in Dorset and Wiltshire which, before changing to mink in 1978, had formerly hunted otter as the Courtenay Tracey Otter Hounds.

It costs almost nothing to go mink-hunting, it provides a pleasant ramble, and no one needs to dress smartly; instead, clothes fit for the rough and tumble of crossing country on foot is the order of the day. The sport is run by genuine 'salt of the earth' country characters and the country would be a poorer place without such people.

Hunting along the River Colne with joint-Master Martin Letts

XV   Hunting Art

THE ARTIST

He stands at no easel, he mixes
no paint,

He colours no canvas to gladden
the eye,

Yet the picture he paints will not fade
or grow faint

Till the love of the chase shall desert
us and die.

He's an artist of parts

Who appeals to the hearts

That can thrill to good hunting and
hounds in full cry.

Will Ogilvie

Mr Edward E. Marshall on his Bay Hunter 'Canada'

by James Lynwood Palmer and Algernon Talmage

Hunting Exercise *by John Emms*

'Doesn't anyone want this picture, even for the frame?' The auctioneer at the country town salesroom was searching for bids in vain. The painting was a large, close-up portrait of two hounds and a terrier resting in their brick-paved kennel, a water brush and a few wisps of straw in front of them, a hunting whip beside. Three pairs of watchful canine eyes appeared to be pleading with me ...

My finger went up. Mine, for £3. (This was in the early 1980s.) There followed a rather faded Lionel Edwards print for £4, worth £40, I was told later, which I also bought.

But it was the copy of John Emms' *Good Companions* that I really loved, and it has graced every hallway of mine since then. Emms (1843–1912) is especially known for his work in the New

Forest, having first gone there to help with the fresco in Lyndhurst parish church. As a keen rider to hounds, it was in the hunting field that he found most of his commissions. He had a natural feeling for the countryside and used strong, free brush strokes. Some critics say his work is too sentimental, but that may be the very reason I like it. Early in the twentieth century he became ill and then destitute, leading the life of a bohemian, and much of his work was taken by village tradesmen in payment of his debts.

Sporting art, especially hunting prints, can be found in most country houses and inns, and many town ones, too. Usually there are racing prints in such houses as well, for the two sports go hand in hand. A prime example is the Horse and Jockey Inn near Thurles in Co. Tipperary, close to the Tipperary, Limerick and Kilkenny Hunts. Here a fine selection of contemporary and eighteenth- and nineteenth-century prints adorn all the walls, as well as many photographs of favourite racehorses, all of them adding to the convivial atmosphere.

The hunting field spawns all manner of different artistic styles and themes. *Hunting Achievements*, painted by Henry Alken and published in print form by Fores Ltd, is a favourite set. The titles alone conjure up the pictures: *Charging an Ox Fence*; *Facing a Brook*; *Swishing a Rasper*; *Topping a flight of rails and coming well into the next field*; *Going along at a Slapping Pace*; and *In and Out Clever*. There are some nostalgic Irish prints, too, such as those 'Dedicated by permission of the most noble the Marquis of Waterford by his lordship's obedient servant,

Brocklesby Ringwood *by George Stubbs*

J. W. Moore. Engraved by G. Hunt and J. R. Mackrel', and dated 1842. Their titles include *The Noble Tips*; *The Marquis at Home*; *Tipperary 'Killing no Murder'*; *Tipperary Boys*; and *Tally Ho to the Sport*.

Henry Alken senior was one of the first artists to portray the hunting field. He was born in 1784 of Danish descent. At first he signed his work 'Ben Tallyho' and soon hunting people were wondering who this artist was who portrayed their sport so well. The secret to his authenticity was that he also rode to hounds. He was a prolific artist in oils and watercolour, of drawings and book illustrations, and much of his work was turned into prints. Many of his hunting pictures show the different sides to jumping; he nearly always painted galloping horses in the one position of all four legs outstretched, as was the custom of the time. It is ironic that he died penniless, for his work adorns countless hundreds of walls. Two of his five children also became artists, Henry Alken junior and Sefferin Alken junior.

George Stubbs is deservedly one of the best regarded painters of the eighteenth century – a reputation well earned through his study and observance of animal anatomy. He portrayed animals as they really were, not stiffly. He could convey not only a lustrous image of the bone, muscle and coat of horse or hound but also the character of the animal through its eyes and head, so that a portrait comes alive to the viewer. Born in 1724 in Liverpool, George Stubbs spent most of his life in London where, through his artistic endeavours, he became patronized by many leading members of the aristocracy. He died in 1806 at the age of eighty-one, and left a superb legacy of his craft.

I have a theory that early hunting landscape artists have much to answer for in perpetuating the myth that followers are nearly always 'in at the death'. The reverse is true, probably the majority never even view a kill, but artistic licence means that the painters like to get as much into one picture as possible. Examples of this are *The Death* by J. F. Herring and *Arriving at the Death* by Henry Alken.

Tally Ho! by Henry Alken

Mr George Marriott on his Bay Hunter Taking a Fence *by John E. Ferneley*

John Frederick Herring (1795–1865) was an artist of Dutch descent who began his career painting crests on coaches; he went on to become Court Painter to Queen Victoria's mother, the Duchess of Kent, and he was also commissioned by the Queen herself.

James Ward (1769–1859) was one of the greatest landscape and animal painters of his era; his *Captain John Levett hunting in the park at Wychnor* is a fine example of a hunting scene in a full landscape.

John E. Ferneley senior (1782–1860) was another who began his career painting coaches. When his talent was spotted, he was sent to London to train under Ben Marshall. After spells in Kent and Ireland, he settled in Melton Mowbray, capital of the hunting world. Although he worked within what was known as the Marshall–Herring tradition, he developed very much his own style. Not only did hunting men and the aristocracy commission him for paintings but so did the renowned Regency dandy Beau Brummell. His portrait of Sir George Marriott on his bay hunter illustrates all the panache and bonhomie of the day.

Moving on a century, another portrait that shows hunting life and style is, unusually, a dually executed painting. James Lynwood Palmer and Algernon Talmage's portrait of Edward E. Marshall on his bay hunter Canada shows the horse stepping out so alertly that you almost feel he will walk out of the canvas at any moment. His owner sits on him with the poise that is born of confidence in an unassuming, relaxed manner. While the

The 6th Earl Winterton, *Sir Alfred Munnings*

horse and rider are a truly eye-catching focal point, there is also a beautifully painted landscape.

James Lynwood Palmer (1868–1941) ran away to Canada, where he worked on ranches for eleven years until his sketches were spotted by an army general who set him on the road to his true vocation. He returned to England in 1899 and, once back, he would ride alongside the horse he was to paint in order to get a feel for it, which he almost tangibly transmitted in to his work.

His collaborator, Algernon Talmage (1871–1939), was also an accomplished equestrian artist, who is particularly remembered for his sensitive portrayal of sunlight, an attribute that is evident in this lovely joint painting.

In the same era, another artist whose work was lifelike thanks to his own prowess in the hunting field was Basil Nightingale (1864–1940). Humour was never far away from him or his work. Exceptionally brave in the saddle, he had much first-hand experience of the dangers and disasters of following hounds, as well as the funny side. He painted Lord Lonsdale, the Yellow Earl, jumping a railway track, and he received a commission from Edward VII. His most well-known work was his portrait of the great Quorn huntsman Tom Firr.

Sir Alfred Munnings painted country and hunting scenes in impressionist style and big, bold portraits on commission. His close-up of a whipper-in and horse brushing through a big, hairy (bullfinch) hedge adorns many walls as a print, while one grey pony finds itself in much of his work. Born in 1878 in Suffolk and a pupil of Norwich Art School, the Royal Academy accepted his first work when he was twenty-one. He became president of the RA in 1944, but resigned five years later after severely criticizing modern artists in a speech attended by his friend Sir Winston Churchill. He died in 1959 at the age of eighty.

'Snaffles' – Charles Johnson Payne (1884–1967) – has been equally as popular for his point-to-point and racing scenes as for his hunting ones, and every painting gives pleasure to look at. Cecil Aldin (1870–1935) was another practical rider to hounds who memorably illustrated the sport, often with a humorous touch.

The twentieth century has spawned some wonderful hunting artists of whom probably the favourite of all is still Lionel Edwards (1878–1966). He evokes the magic of hunting and its landscapes so realistically that the viewer can imagine himself there in the picture. Many of his paintings have been made into prints and he also illustrated many books. One of his protégés was John King who, along with artists such as Peter Biegel, Michael

The Finest View in Europe by Charles Johnstone 'Snaffles' Payne

THE FINEST VIEW IN EUROPE

And there down hill three fields ahead
A lolloping dog-fox sped

(Reynard the Fox)

The Quorn Running Towards Quenby Hall *by Lionel Edwards*

Lyne, Malcolm Coward, Neil Cawthorne, Daniel Crane, Elizabeth Scrivenour, whose specialty is hounds, and Irish-based Peter Curling, portrays many different hunting scenes today with an aptitude that makes one long to collect them all.

In the end it all boils down to choice, not so much of artist as of individual picture. Often the only way to acquire such work is through a print, an art form that is still flourishing, and limited editions of favourite works continue to be collected keenly. Coloured etchings had begun to be made in Switzerland in the eighteenth century by Johann Ludwig Aberlie and provided the means by which the less well-off could afford to buy realistic replicas of the real thing; they have stood the test of time.

One whose business it is to select a suitable work and then to see that it is reproduced faithfully is Sally Mitchell from Nottinghamshire. All Sally ever wanted to do from the age of five was to ride horses but when she came to working age, her father protested and sent her off to London. There, her natural dealing instincts – she used to buy sale rejects and turn them into foxhunter ponies – led her to the major auction houses, but not before she had been a stunt rider in one or two films and had tried her hand at selling jewellery.

It was a sporting art sale at Sotheby's that got her hooked. She began acquiring pictures, but they were too expensive for many people to buy. The niche market was in prints. A successful change of direction followed an approach from country dog and equine artist John Trickett. Once all the checking procedures have been carried out – 'quality is so important' – the artist then signs the prints. If they sell out, they can be expected to increase in value over time.

No glimpse of hunting art would be complete without an inclusion of photography and a man who has made this art form his own, Jim Meads. Now turned seventy, he has been known for more than fifty years as 'the running photographer', and has photographed a staggering 454 different packs of hounds worldwide.

An all-round sportsman and accomplished cricketer, Jim Meads followed the Enfield Chace (now amalgamated with the Cambridgeshire) as 'often as money allowed' as a schoolboy and before long he was photographing a number of local packs. What has set him apart from other photographers has been the willingness to leave behind the easy option by road and take to running across the fields, no matter how arduous or tiring the going underfoot. He once received a letter from Jacqueline Kennedy Onassis expressing astonishment at the speed with which he crossed country on foot. In latter years, America has become a frequent stamping-ground for him and his camera.

He began photographing with an old-fashioned plate camera and says that although he has seen much else change in the world, 'fox-hunting, hare hunting, stag-hunting and, in America, coyote hunting go from strength to strength, giving tremendous pleasure to tens of thousands of ordinary people. Long may it continue, so that new generations can thrill to the sound of the horn and hounds in full cry, in pursuit of their natural quarry in their natural environment, despite man's attempt to spoil it.'

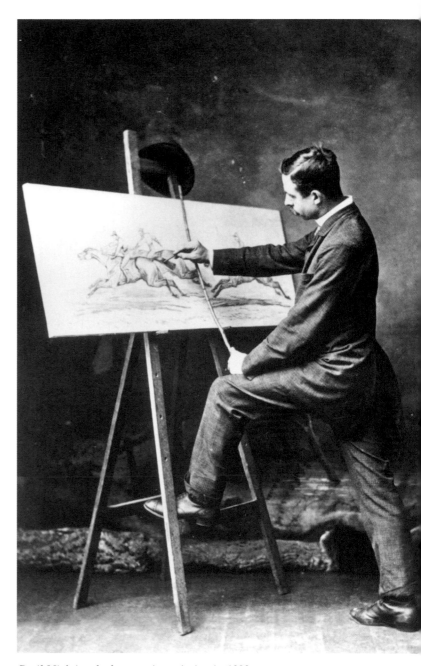

Basil Nightingale, horse artist, painting in 1892

XVI Hunting Literature

Visit any hunting book collector, and the sheer range of books is immediately apparent, from the practical guides to the hunt histories, biographies and colourful fiction, all from the eighteenth century to the twenty-first.

Young lady (in a hurry) 'Have you bought the gap sir, or only taken it on lease?' *by G. H. Jalland, from* The Sporting Adventures of Mr Popple

Favourites can swing according to mood, a collector told me. As an all-time favourite, he plumped for the post-war edition of the annual *Bailey's Hunting Directory* (a one-off edition covering 1939–49). 'It showed the courage and humour that is inherent in the hunting world, and everything that hunting stands for,' he said, 'and it included a roll of honour of all those hunt servants and masters of hounds who were killed in service. They died for our freedom and rights.'

Of the many practical books on hunting, the best known by far is Peter Beckford's *Thoughts on Hunting*, penned in 1779. After more than 200 years it remains the foxhunter's bible on dos and don'ts. Written as a series of letters to a young man wishing

to start hunting, it concentrates on the hounds and those who hunt and care for them, rather than the horses and followers, though there are pertinent tips for them, too, such as not crowding in on hounds.

Peter Beckford was born in 1740 and grew up on the Steepleton estate outside Blandford Forum in Dorset. The estate

Hold Back, Sir! *by Cecil Aldin*

was bought by Peter's father, Julines, from Thomas Fownes who, in 1730, was responsible for the first organized hunting in Dorset of fox, deer and marten cats. As a boy, Peter often used to take a few hounds up on to Cranbourne Chase and, after a particularly good foxhunt one day, Peter vowed to kennel a pack at Steepleton once his education was complete. This he did, at the age of twenty-three, and built up a good pack of hounds and a fine reputation for himself as Master and huntsman. In 1781 the first edition of his *Thoughts on Hunting* was published and in 1804 he presented a copy to young J. J. Farquaharson, who went on to hunt the whole of Dorset for fifty years before it was split into the Portman, South Dorset, Cattistock and Blackmore Vale Hunts between 1857 and 1859. Peter Beckford, a cousin of the Lord Mayor of London William Beckford, married a daughter of Lord Rivers, had one son, and died in 1810 at the age of fifty, but even nearly ninety years later, in 1899, there were seven editions of his standard work printed that year alone.

For those who like something short and straightforward as a blueprint, they can do no better than keep a copy of *36 Tips to a Huntsman*, which is written in such a way that they are, in effect, rules. Cecil Aldin, better known as an artist, wrote *Ratcatcher to Scarlet* (1926), another 'how-to' book, between the wars in the form of a series of letters to his son-in-law and the 'young entry' everywhere. It is copiously illustrated throughout in both line drawings and colour. Two large books from the same era, *Forrard On!* and *Tally-Ho Back*, by 'Rancher' are written entirely in verse and superbly illustrated with drawings by Lionel Edwards.

Also in verse is the four-book poem called *The Chace, a Poem* by William Somervile, first published in 1735. Somervile was born in Warwickshire in 1677 and elected a scholar to Winchester College in 1690. From there he went up to New College, Oxford, where he became a fellow. He spent most of his holidays enjoying field sports, especially 'the chase'. According to R. Farquharson Sharp, in his memoir of the author which prefaces the 1896 edition, in the garden of his home Somervile built a well-sheltered kennel by the millstream and kennelled twelve couple of beagles, bred chiefly between the small Cotswold harrier and the Southern hound; six couple of foxhounds, rather rough and wire-haired; and five couple of otterhounds, which in the winter season made an addition to the foxhounds. He kept no more than four horses, of which his favourite, Old Ball, often hunted three times a week. Old Ball 'was a real good English hunter, standing about fifteen hands high, with black legs, short back, high in the shoulders, large barrel, thin head, cropped ears, and a white blaze down the face.'

THE CHACE

The chace I sing, hounds and their various breed,
And no less various use. O thou great prince!
Whom Cambria's tow'ring hills proclaim their lord,
Deign thou to hear my bold, instructive song.
While grateful citizens, with pompous shew,
Rear the triumphal arch, rich with th' exploits
Of thy illustrious house; while virgins pave
Thy way with flow'rs, and, as the royal youth
Passing they view, admire, and sigh in vain;
While crowded theatres, too fondly proud
Of their exotic minstrels and shrill pipes,
The price of manhood, hail thee with a song,
And airs soft-warbling; my hoarse-sounding horn
Invites thee to the chace, the sport of kings;
Image of war, without its guilt. The Muse
Aloft on wing shall soar, conduct with care
Thy foaming courser o'er the steepy rock,
Or on the river bank receive thee safe,
Light-bounding o'er the wave, from shore to shore.
Be thou our great protector, gracious youth!
And if, in future times, some envious prince,
Careless of right and guileful, should invade
Thy Britain's commerce, or should strive in vain

To wrest the balance from thy equal hand;
Thy hunter-train, in cheerful green array'd
(A band undaunted and inur'd to toils),
Shall compass thee around, die at thy feet,
Or hew thy passage thro' th' embattled foe,
And clear thy way to fame; inspir'd by thee,
The nobler chace of glory shall pursue
Thro' fire, and smoke, and blood, and fields of death.

Nature, in her productions slow, aspires
By just degrees to reach perfection's height:
So mimic art works leisurely, till time
Improve the piece, or wise experience give
The proper finishing. When Nimrod bold,
That mighty hunter, first made war on beasts,
And stain'd the wood-land green with purple dye,
New, and unpolish'd was the huntsman's art;
No stated rule, his wanton will his guide.

… And if, to crown my joys,
Ye grant me health, that, ruddy in my cheeks,
Blooms in my life's decline; fields, woods, and streams,
Each tow'ring hill, each humble vale below,
Shall hear my cheering voice, my hounds shall wake
The lazy morn, and glad th' horizon round.

William Somervile

The success of *The Chace* was immediate and it was reprinted many times over more than a hundred years. I have chosen its opening lines and ending for inclusion here. Dr Johnson, known as a severe critic of verse, said the poem was written 'with great intelligence of his subject, which is the first requisite to excellence'. Another critic wrote, 'Of all books on hunting, this alone

The Chace *taken from* The Chace, A Poem,
illustrated by Hugh Thomson

seems to describe "sport" in its true meaning, and is a great deal more correct in details than any modern books I ever read.' Peter Beckford, born five years after its publication, unashamedly drew upon it for his *Thoughts on Hunting*. In his first letter, he wrote, 'When I have any better authority than my own, such as Somervile, for instance (who by the bye, is the only one that has written intelligibly on this subject), I shall take the liberty of giving it you in his own words, to save you the trouble of turning to him.'

John Masefield's narrative poem 'Reynard the Fox' (1919) remains popular. Siegfried Sassoon's poetry was mostly anti-war but an enduring prose favourite is his still-popular *Memoirs of a Fox-Hunting Man* (1928), a 'must' for hunting aficionados.

Many of the books written prior to the Second World War have mysterious authors and long-winded subtitles. Although the style differs greatly from the present day, most are gems to read. People will have personal reasons for selecting their favourites. One might be *Hold Hard! Hounds Please! A discourse on the foxhound in the field, covert and kennel, with hunting yarns, character sketches from life, and some notes on breeding and kennel treatment* by Yoi Over (a pseudonym for the author, who was huntsman and whipper-in to many well-known packs for over forty years. 'Yoi over' is the hunting term for the fox having crossed the ride), which was published in 1924. Some of its chapters include the craft of the huntsman; the whipper-in and his job; earthstopper; kennelman; scent; and hound characteristics. Another is called *The Life of a Fox*, written by himself by Thomas Smith, late Master of the Craven and at present of the Pytchley, 1920. It includes coloured plates after Henry Alken and others.

Many hunting memoirs have been written, including *Try Back, Being 33 years of a Huntsman's Reminiscences* by A. Henry Higginson, MFH, 1932, which includes two forewords. One is by

John Jorrocks with his celebrated hunter Arterxerxes, from
John Jorrocks and Other Characters by Gerald French,
illustrated by the Earl of Ypres

Ikey Bell, the great American-born huntsman and hound breeder of such packs as the Galway Blazers, the Kilkenny and the South and West Wilts (see pp. 100–1), in which he recalls the fear he felt in crossing the Atlantic shortly after the *Titantic* disaster. Of artist Lionel Edwards, with whom he stayed, he wrote, 'he is charming, a finished horseman and a sporting painter who to my mind is unequalled at the present time.'

Ikey Bell also wrote the foreword to the 1930 book, *The Foxhunting Reminiscences of 'Gin & Beer'*, the pseudonym of one Tom Andrews, who dedicated the book 'respectfully to Lord and Lady Charles Bentink in pleasant remembrance of the happy five years during which Lord Charles was Master of the Croome Hounds'. In it he tells some amusing tales of hunting in and around Worcestershire. Another book from this period is entitled *To Whom the Goddess, Hunting and Riding for Women* by Lady Diana Sheddon and Lady Apsley, 1932.

Reminiscences of a Huntsman by the Hon. Grantley F. Berkeley, 1854, is illustrated with delightful line drawings by Leech. Another memoir is *A Master of Hounds, being the Life Story of Harry Buckland of Ashford by One Who Knows Him*, 1931. My own favourite is *A Famous Fox-hunter: Reminiscences of the late Thomas Assheton Smith, or the Pursuits of an English Country Gentleman* by John E. Eardley-Wilmot (1859), who lived in Tedworth House (now owned by the army) on the Hampshire–Wiltshire borders, from where he ran the Tedworth Hunt, with whom I spent several very happy seasons.

The same sort of reasoning probably accounts for taste in the numerous hunt histories, too, though all of them reveal a fascinating glimpse of social history.

Among many are *The Wynnstay Country* by T. H. G. Puleston, 'printed for private circulation only', 1893; *The Pytchley Hunt Past and Present* by the late H. O. Nethercote, for fifty years a member of this famous hunt, 1888; and *The Eridge Hunt* by Henry S. Eeles, 1936.

Then there is hunting fiction, in particular the stories of John Jorrocks from the pen of R. S. Surtees. Robert Smith Surtees, born in 1805, was a lightweight novelist compared to his contemporary, Charles Dickens, and used a much smaller canvas, that of the hunting world. But where he did score was, like Dickens, in having an eye for and poking fun at the foibles, the strengths and the weaknesses of human nature, often in highly amusing form.

He created the cockney grocer Jorrocks, whose ambition he fulfilled to bear the letters MFH (Master of Foxhounds) after his name, and whose fictional name is known among a far wider audience than the hunting one alone. The character even spawned a West End musical of the name, starring Joss Acland in the lead role, in the 1970s, more than a hundred years after he was invented.

It was Jorrocks who said, "Unting is all that's worth living for – all time is lost wot is not spent in 'unting – it is like the hair we breathe – if we have it not we die – it's the sport of kings, the image of war without its guilt, and only five-and-twenty per cent of its danger' (*Handley Cross*, 1843).

Jorrocks' favourite poem was Somervile's *The Chace*, from which Surtees borrowed the phrase 'the image of war without its guilt' for his novel. A few more well-loved quotes from Surtees' pen are: 'Three things I never lends – my 'oss, my wife, and my name' (*Hillingdon Hall*, 1845); 'Women never look so well as when one comes in wet and dirty from hunting' (Mr Sponge's Sporting Tour, 1853); 'There is no secret so close as that between a rider and his horse' (*Mr Sponge's Sporting Tour*); 'The only infallible rule we know is, that the man who is always talking about being a gentleman never is one' (*Ask Mamma*, 1858); 'More people are flattered into virtue than bullied out of vice' (*The Analysis of the Hunting Field*, 1846); and, 'It ar'n't that I loves the fox less, but that I loves the 'ound more' (*Handley Cross*).

Other favourite Surtees novels down the generations include *Jorrocks' Jaunts and Jollities* (1838); *Mr Facey Romford's Hounds* (published in 1865, a year after his death); and *Plain or Ringlets?* (1860) among others. Surtees' writing spanned a quarter of a century until his death at the age of fifty-nine.

At the end of the century, we have the less frivolous but equally humorous twosome: *The Irish RM: Some Experiences of an Irish RM* (1899) and *Further Experiences of an Irish RM* (1908), written by Somerville and Ross. Edith Somerville and Violet Ross were Irish cousins who collaborated for a dozen works of fiction based on the hunting world, usually of Anglo-Irish estate owners, at the turn of the twentieth century. One hundred years later, their work was much enjoyed when it was made into a television series in 1989.

It might, unfortunately, be politically incorrect to write hunting fiction today, but luckily there is a stack of good yarns that have survived down the generations and are read just as avidly now as they were a century or so ago. *One is A Long Way to Go* by Marigold Armitage, 1952, a light novel and delightful tale of country romance and hunting life in Ireland in the first half of the twentieth century. At one point, the narrator has been describing his parents' move to Ireland from England and how the first thing they did was add extra bathrooms and install central heating, enabling the writer, after a day's hunting, to luxuriate in heat and steam steeped in the smell of pine essence and rolling the Jameson around his tongue.

He goes on to say, 'Now there are lots of warm houses, because of the refugees. Very seldom indeed in history can refugees have been invariably associated with centrally-heated houses; yet so it was in Southern Ireland at this time, with the refugees from super-tax, State medicine, milk marketing board returns, and General Interference flooding the land, lending their glorious be-collared presences to the hunts, being done by friendly cattle dealers and varying between intense adoration and extreme dislike of the native's belief in magic, unscientific farming, dirt, funerals and the Pope.'

Now, at the start of the twenty-first century, I have moved to a delightful rural part of Ireland, thus joining a new band of refugees fleeing much the same sort of interference and discovering anew the magic of this land. Plus ça change.

Facey Romford and Lucy Glitters (alias Mrs Somerville) returning from hunting from John Jorrocks and Other Characters *by Gerald French, illustrated by the Earl of Ypres*

XVII   Tailpiece

Sunny was the 'wrong' colour and

breed for hunting, being palomino and

part-bred Arab, but he hunted 335

days, and jumped over 1,000 team chase

fences: he was the hunter of my life.

Anne Holland jumping on Sunny

'GOODNIGHT, PAL'

For his thirteenth consecutive Opening Meet in 1996 – Grafton seven, South Dorset six – he was, as usual, on his toes. Hunting conditions were difficult, but there is nothing like the anticipation of a new season, so, in spite of the wind and rain, Sunny (Colebridge Miralgo) was raring to go.

Before long his extravagant jumping was drawing gasps from the foot-followers and, at one time, for a few magical moments, we were alone with hounds. Sunny was disgusted with me for leaving at 2.40, regardless of the rain and howling gale. Never mind, I thought, there's the whole season ahead of us …

Twelve years earlier a friend had found me at the back of the field, tears of frustration welling, because Sunny wouldn't jump a place barely 18 inches high. Soon after, I sold him. Fate intervened, for three days later he was returned, having spent 72 hours chasing his intended companions round and round their field.

It was the same friend who, after Sunny's first night turned out at summer grass, phoned at 7 a.m. to say he had been caught in a cattle grid and needed a vet. 'I'm afraid you'll have to ask him to bring a gun,' he added. Sunny bore the scars permanently, but the only time he ever got angry was when he was deprived of his male parts. A stallion with progeny, five years was painfully late for the operation.

His only other serious accident also occurred at grass, when an unshod 12hh pony kicked his forearm and severed an artery. Awash with free-flowing blood, his life was saved by the prompt application of a tourniquet.

Once Sunny got his jumping act together, it was always flamboyant. He cleared fences by feet rather than by inches so that we literally soared in mid-air. If he was 'wrong' or frightened, he would stop; he never hit a jump. Fleet of foot (he briefly Arab raced) and blessed with legs of iron, abundant stamina and the biggest heart, as well as movement that floated across the ground, he could have been a top endurance or dressage horse, but I don't believe he would have swapped his hunting/team-chasing/summer-at-grass life for anything.

In team chases, the cross-country events run by different hunts in spring and autumn, a conservative estimate for Sunny of five runs a year for ten years jumping an average of twenty fences comes to 1,000 fences. Our years with the Roadrunners can only be described as hilarious fun. Formed by four hunting friends and our hunters, we once even qualified for and ran in the National Championships. And there is on tape a commentator's remark at the Atherstone, 'I'd give my eye teeth for a day's hunting on this palomino; his style reminds me of Sunsalve …'

It is as a hunter that Sunny will be remembered. My last diary entry about him in November 1996 reads: 'Sunny felt absolutely brilliant'; the first one, in September 1984: 'a pleasant morning's cubbing and a good introduction for Sunny'. I have many recollections in between, some in fog, others in bottomless ground or with poor scent. There are the memories of giving my son, George, his first day in the Vale, and Charmian Hill, Dawn Run's owner, her only English hunting, or that day in his second season when things suddenly clicked into place for him. On a 1986 visit to the West Country, my diary records: 'Taunton Vale, huge ditches and hedges, very high iron gate, little fall in a ditch but very good over black fences; middle hunt hard and long with hounds flying …'

The 1989–90 season was his busiest: thirty-nine occasions behind hounds, and each time he came out bouncing for more. A run of 1 ½ hours in rain and plough is recorded, my diary ending with the note, 'Sunny such a super ride'. Later in December, after several days hard frost, 'Sunny knew it was slippery, jumped badly, and stopped me off on the team chase course!' – such was his intelligence and sense of humour.

He was capable of teasing novice riders and tearing off with them, but he always stopped when it mattered. He hated being left behind on hunting days and would do the equivalent of two days' pacing up and down by the field gate or 'tap dancing' in his box, and whinnied with joy on reunion when the lorry returned, carrying the horse that had gone hunting without him.

There were Melton Hunt Club visits to Leicestershire with him, too, but it is the Beaufort visit, more than anything, that stands out. It was the retirement of Brian Gupwell, who had hunted the Eridge hounds after the retirement of Bob Field-Marsham in my childhood, and well-wishers had come from far and wide, making a sea of different coat colours. (Brian sadly died in 2002.) What fun it was to watch the fox leave Icehouse Pond, lope past the famous lake and run along the front of Badminton House. From there we jumped in and out of Luckington Lane, over Tom Smith's walls and the hedges that form the Aintree fences in the Big Event; all the while Sunny was in his element. The day ended with hounds pulling down their quarry at Brian's feet, enabling him to blow the kill for the last time in his distinguished career.

But for all the good runs, cheerful camaraderie of the hunting field and memorable visits, nothing was more magical than standing on point alone on Sunny. Suddenly, I would feel his heart quicken, his head come up, ears pricked, body taut and eyes following Charlie's stealthy movement; once again, he had seen the fox first. Ah, that heart – a heart fit to burst.

One day, feeling he was not himself as we moved off from a lovely meet, I led him back to the horsebox. As we approached, hounds were in full cry in the nearby covert; Sunny's head came up, a little spring came back into his step, and his heart pounded. It was still pounding when the vet arrived at home, but at midnight he was calm. He gave me a little knicker and he was warm and had eaten his supper. I put my arms around his neck and hugged him, not in foreboding, simply love. Some time in the early hours he died. So, no dreaded gun, no agonizing decision, but the lucky way. The hounds of heaven had called.

Goodnight, pal. And thanks.

THE HORSE OF YOUR HEART

When you've ridden a four-year-old half of the day
And, foam to the fetlock, they lead him away,
With a sigh of contentment you watch him depart
While you tighten the girths on the horse of your heart.

There is something between you that both understand
As it thrills an old message from bit-bar to hand.
As he changes his feet in that plunge of desire
To the thud of his hoofs all your courage takes fire.

When an afternoon fox is away, when begins
The rush down the headland that edges the whins,
When you challenge the Field, making sure of a start,
Would you ask any horse but this horse of your heart?

There's the rasping big double a green one would shirk,
But the old fellow knows it as part of his work;
He has shortened his stride, he has measured the task,
He is up, on, and over and clean as you'd ask.

There's the water before you – no novice's test,
But a jump to try deeply the boldest and best;
Just a tug at the leather, a lift of the ear,
And the old horse is over it – twenty foot clear.

There is four foot of wall and a take-off in plough,
And you're glad you are riding no tenderfoot now
But a seasoned campaigner, a master of art,
The perfect performer, the horse of your heart.

For here's where the raw one will falter and baulk,
And here's where the tyro is pulled to a walk,
But the horse of your heart never dwells or demurs
And is over the top to a touch of the spurs.

To you who ride young ones half-schooled and half-broke,
What joy to find freedom a while from your yoke!
What bliss to be launched with the luck of the start
On the old one, the proved one, the horse of your heart!

Will Ogilvie

Credits

My grateful thanks to the following for the use of their pictures:

Anne Alcock
Pages: 30, 62

Kevill Armstrong
Page: 96

Bridgeman Art Library
Page 164: Bonhams, London, UK/Bridgeman Art Library
Pages 166–7: Christie's Images, London, UK/Bridgeman Art Library
Page 169: Private Collection/Christie's Images/Bridgeman Art Library
Page 172, 176: Yale Center for British Art, Paul Mellon Collection, USA/Photo: Bridgeman Art Library

Camera Press
Page: 35

EMPICS
Pages: 1, 128, 161

Mary Evans Picture Library
Pages: 2, 27, 41, 42–3, 60–1

Jim Meads
Pages: 13, 14, 16, 18, 28, 31, 39, 50, 52, 53, 56, 64–5, 67, 68, 74, 76, 78, 80–1, 84, 86, 88, 90, 91, 95, 100, 102, 104, 105, 107, 109, 110, 111, 112–13, 114, 116, 118, 119, 122, 130, 146–7, 148, 149, 150–1, 152, 154–5, 158–9

Des McCheane
Pages: 120, 121, 123, 124–5, 126, 127, 129, 131, 132, 135

Michael Osman
Pages: 87, 89

Barbara Thomson
Page: 141

Sotheby's
Pages: 36–7, 98–9, 162–3, 170–1

E. Walsh
Page: 108

My own pictures appear on pages: 24, 138, 142–3, 157, 184–5

Every effort has been made to trace copyright holders of the illustrative material included in this book, but if any have been inadvertently overlooked, the publisher will be pleased to make the necessary arrangements at the first opportunity.